CLOUD 9

Other plays by CARYL CHURCHILL also available
Traps
Fen
Top Girls
Vinegar Tom (included in *Plays by Women, Volume 1*)
Softcops

CLOUD 9

REVISED AMERICAN EDITION

by Caryl Churchill

Routledge
New York

First published in the United States of America in 1984 by Methuen, Inc.
733 Third Avenue, New York, N.Y. 10017
First published in Great Britain by Pluto Press Limited and Joint Stock
Theatre Group in 1979
Second Edition 1980
Reprinted 1981
Third Edition 1983
Fourth Edition (Revised) 1984
Reprinted in U.S.A. 1985
Reprinted in U.S.A. 1987
Reprinted in U.S.A. 1991
Reprinted in U.S.A. 1992 by Routledge
Reprinted in U.S.A. 1994 by Routledge
Reprinted in U.S.A. 1995 by Routledge
Reprinted in U.S.A. 1996 by Routledge

Reprinted in U.S.A. 1998 by Routledge,
an imprint of Routledge, Chapman and Hall, Inc.
29 West 35 Street, New York, N.Y. 10001

Library of Congress Cataloging in Publication Data

Churchill, Caryl.
  Cloud Nine.

   I. Title.
PR6053.H786C5   1984   822'.914   83-26421
ISBN 0-415-90135-9 (pbk.)

Lyrics *Come Gather Sons of England* copyright Anthony Wilkin 1902
    A Boy's Best Friend copyright Joseph D. Skelly 1897
    Cloud Nine copyright © Caryl Churchill/Andy Roberts 1979

Music available from Andy Roberts c/o Roger Hancock, Ltd.,
8 Waterloo Place, Pall Mall, London SW1

Cloud 9 was first performed at Dartington College of Arts on February 14, 1979 by the Joint Stock Theatre Group.

The revised edition was first performed at the Royal Court Theatre, August 30, 1980, in a co-production with Joint Stock.

ACT I

	JOINT STOCK	*ROYAL COURT*
Clive	*Anthony Sher*	*Graeme Garden*
Betty	*Jim Hooper*	*Ron Cook*
Joshua	*Tony Rohr*	*Anthony O'Donnell*
Edward	*Julie Covington*	*Harriet Walter*
Maud	*Miriam Margolies*	*Anna Nigh*
Ellen/Mrs. S	*Carole Hayman*	*Maggie Steed*
Harry Bagley	*William Hoyland*	*Hugh Fraser*

ACT II

Betty	*Julie Covington*	*Maggie Steed*
Edward	*Jim Hooper*	*Graeme Garden*
Victoria	*Miriam Margolies*	*Harriet Walter*
Martin	*William Hoyland*	*Hugh Fraser*
Lin	*Carole Hayman*	*Anna Nigh*
Cathy	*Anthony Sher*	*Anthony O'Donnell*
Gerry	*Tony Rohr*	*Ron Cook*

Director: Max Stafford-Clark
Assistant Director and Co-director: Les Waters
Designer: Peter Hartwell
Musical Director: Andy Roberts
Lighting Designer: Robin Myerscough-Walker

Cloud 9 opened in New York on May 18, 1981 at the Lucille Lortel Theatre, produced by Michel Stuart and Harvey J. Klaris in association with Michel Kleinman Productions.

The cast was as follows:

ACT I

Clive	*Jeffrey Jones*
Betty	*Zjelko Ivanek*
Joshua	*Don Amendolia*
Edward	*Concetta Tomei*
Maud	*Veronica Castang*
Ellen/Mrs. S	*E. Katherine Kerr*
Harry Bagley	*Nicolas Surovy*

ACT II

Betty	*E. Katherine Kerr*
Edward	*Jeffrey Jones*
Victoria	*Concetta Tomei*
Martin	*Nicolas Surovy*
Lin	*Veronica Castang*
Cathy	*Don Amendolia*
Gerry	*Zjelko Ivanek*

Director: Tommy Tune
Sets: Lawrence Miller
Costumes: Michel Stuart and Gene London
Lighting: Marcia Madeira
Title Song and Incidental Music: Maury Yeston
Sound: Warren Hogan

Cloud Nine was written for Joint Stock Theatre Group in 1979. I had worked with them before (LIGHT SHINING IN BUCK-INGHAMSHIRE 1976 directed by Max Stafford-Clark) and have since (FEN 1983 directed by Les Waters).

Joint Stock was founded in 1974 by Max Stafford-Clark, William Gaskell, David Hare and David Aukin. The actors are not a permanent company, though many of the same people have appeared in several productions. Occasionally the company has produced a play that was already written (e.g. VICTORY by Howard Barker 1983) or devised a play without a writer (YES-TERDAY'S NEWS 1976, AN OPTIMISTIC THRUST 1981); but the most usual method of work is for writer, director and actors to spend three or four weeks on a workshop, researching the subject (often taken from a book, e.g. David Hare's FAN SHEN 1975, Stephen Lowe's RAGGED TROUSERED PHILAN-THROPISTS 1978) and for the writer then to go off for about ten weeks to write the play. There is then a six week rehearsal, which gives time for the writer to revise the script, often in consultation with the company, and the show then plays for twelve weeks—four on tour, four in London, four on tour again.

As the starting point for the CLOUD NINE workshop I suggested to Max Stafford-Clark simply "sexual politics" rather than any book, an unnervingly general subject which soon became specific. We formed a company considering their sexual as well as acting experience. With LIGHT SHINING the workshop was concerned with researching a historical period remote from us and then finding how we related to it, whereas with CLOUD NINE we started from ourselves, moving out from that to a more general context. Then I went away and wrote the play. I originally thought it would all be set in the present like the second act; but the idea of colonialism as a parallel to sexual oppression, which I first came across in Genet, had been briefly touched on in the workshop. When I thought of the colonial setting the whole thing fell quite quickly into place. Though no character is based on anyone in the company, the play draws deeply on our experiences, and would not have been written without the workshop.

There were no black members of the company and this led me to the idea of Joshua being so alienated from himself and so much aspiring to be what white men want him to be that he is played by a white. Similarly, Betty, who has no more respect for women than Joshua has for blacks, and who wants to be what men want her to be, is played by a man. For Edward to be played by a woman is within the English tradition of women playing boys (e.g. PETER PAN); for Cathy to be played by a man is a simple reversal of this. Of course, for both that reversal highlights how much they have to be taught to be society's idea of a little boy and girl.

The doubling in the original production was Clive-Cathy, Betty-Edward, Edward-Betty, Maud-Victoria, Ellen/Mrs. Saunders-Lin, Joshua-Gerry, Harry-Martin. The London run was at the Royal Court Theatre, and a year later, 1980, the Royal Court and Joint Stock revived the play, directed by Max Stafford-Clark and Les Waters, with a different cast and with this doubling: Clive-Edward, Betty-Gerry, Edward-Victoria, Maud-Lin, Ellen/Mrs. Saunders-Betty, Joshua-Cathy, and again Harry-Martin. This was partly to fit the parts to the different actors and partly to give us all a chance to try something new. Different doublings throw up different resonances. I have a weakness for Clive-Cathy. Betty-Edward, Edward-Betty, throws an interesting emphasis on that relationship, while Betty-Gerry gives Betty her chance to be dangerous. In the second version the same couples reappear: Clive and Betty become Edward and Gerry, Edward and Harry become Victoria and Martin. And so on—there is no right way, just various interesting possibilities.

The second production was seen by Michel Stuart, who produced the play in New York at the Theatre de Lys (now the Lucille Lortel Theatre) directed by Tommy Tune. We made a few changes in the text: some cuts, mainly in Act I, Scene 3, a few lines restored from an earlier version, slight alterations in the appearances in Act II of characters from Act I, and, the only structural change, moved Betty's monologue from earlier in the scene to after her scene with Gerry, just before the end. I enjoyed working with Tune and trying different things, and am now left with the difficulty of deciding what text should be published. There is a lot that is attractive about the New York ending, and it provides more of an emotional climax, which is why we did it. But on the whole I prefer the play not to end with Betty's self discovery but with her moving beyond that to a first attempt to make a new relationship with someone else. So I have left the speech in its original position. Other small changes: the original song at the end of Act II, Scene 3 was cut and replaced by a new song, not sung by the company, at the end of the play; the Victorian song "A Boy's Best Friend" was cut from the end of Act I, Scene 3; and Cathy was originally on a swing, not bouncing a ball. For this edition I have kept some changes that were made for New York while often keeping to the original. Sometimes the decision was difficult as I am very fond of both productions. But in any case the differences are quite small, and almost imperceptible to anyone less close to the play than I am.

Caryl Churchill

CLOUD 9

CHARACTERS

ACT I

Clive
Betty, *his wife, played by a man*
Joshua, *his black servant, played by a white*
Edward, *his son, played by a woman*
Victoria, *his daughter, a dummy*
Maud, *his mother-in-law*
Ellen, *Edward's governess*
Harry Bagley, *an explorer*
Mrs. Saunders, *a widow*

ACT II

Betty
Edward, *her son*
Victoria, *her daughter*
Martin, *Victoria's husband*
Lin
Cathy, *Lin's daughter age 5, played by a man*
Gerry, *Edward's lover*

Except for Cathy, characters in Act II are played
   by actors of their own sex.

Act I takes place in a British colony in Africa
   in Victorian times.

Act II takes place in London in the present,
   but for the characters it is twenty-five years later.

ACT ONE

ACT I

Scene 1

*Low bright sun. Verandah. Flagpole with Union
Jack.*
The Family—CLIVE, BETTY, EDWARD, VICTORIA, MAUD,
ELLEN, JOSHUA.

ALL *(sung)*
    Come gather, sons of England, come gather in your
        pride,
    Now meet the world united, now face it side by side;
    Ye who the earth's wide corners, from veldt to prai-
        rie, roam.
    From bush and jungle muster all who call old En-
        gland 'home'.

    Then gather round for England,
    Rally to the flag,
    From North and South and East and West
    Come one and all for England!

CLIVE
    This is my family. Though far from home
    We serve the Queen wherever we may roam
    I am a father to the natives here,
    And father to my family so dear.

He presents Betty. She is played by a man.

    My wife is all I dreamt a wife should be,

And everything she is she owes to me.

BETTY

> I live for Clive. The whole aim of my life
> Is to be what he looks for in a wife.
> I am a man's creation as you see,
> And what men want is what I want to be.

Clive presents Joshua. He is played by a white.

CLIVE

> My boy's a jewel. Really has the knack.
> You'd hardly notice that the fellow's black.

JOSHUA

> My skin is black but oh my soul is white.
> I hate my tribe. My master is my light.
> I only live for him. As you can see,
> What white men want is what I want to be.

Clive presents Edward. He is played by a woman.

CLIVE

> My son is young. I'm doing all I can
> To teach him to grow up to be a man.

EDWARD

> What father wants I'd dearly like to be.
> I find it rather hard as you can see.

Clive presents Victoria, who is a dummy, Maud, and Ellen.

CLIVE

> No need for any speeches by the rest.
> My daughter, mother-in-law, and governess.

ALL *(sung)*

> O'er countless numbers she, our Queen,
> Victoria reigns supreme;
> O'er Afric's sunny plains, and o'er

Canadian frozen stream;
The forge of war shall weld the chains of brother-
    hood secure;
So to all time in ev'ry clime our Empire shall en-
    dure.

Then gather round for England,
Rally to the flag,
From North and South and East and West
Come one and all for England!

All go except Betty.

Clive comes.

BETTY Clive?

CLIVE Betty. Joshua!

Joshua comes with a drink for Clive.

BETTY I thought you would never come. The day's so long
    without you.

CLIVE Long ride in the bush.

BETTY Is anything wrong? I heard drums.

CLIVE Nothing serious. Beauty is a damned good mare. I
    must get some new boots sent from home. These ones
    have never been right. I have a blister.

BETTY My poor dear foot.

CLIVE It's nothing.

BETTY Oh but it's sore.

CLIVE We are not in this country to enjoy ourselves. Must
    have ridden fifty miles. Spoke to three different

headmen who would all gladly chop off each other's heads and wear them round their waists.

BETTY Clive!

CLIVE Don't be squeamish, Betty, let me have my joke. And what has my little dove done today?

BETTY I've read a little.

CLIVE Good. Is it good?

BETTY It's poetry.

CLIVE You're so delicate and sensitive.

BETTY And I played the piano. Shall I send for the children?

CLIVE Yes, in a minute. I've a piece of news for you.

BETTY Good news?

CLIVE You'll certainly think it's good. A visitor.

BETTY From home?

CLIVE No. Well of course originally from home.

BETTY Man or woman?

CLIVE Man.

BETTY I can't imagine.

CLIVE Something of an explorer. Bit of a poet. Odd chap but brave as a lion. And a great admirer of yours.

BETTY What do you mean? Whoever can it be?

CLIVE With an H and a B. And does conjuring tricks for little Edward.

BETTY That sounds like Mr. Bagley.

CLIVE Harry Bagley.

BETTY He certainly doesn't admire me, Clive, what a thing to say. How could I possibly guess from that. He's hardly explored anything at all, he's just been up a river, he's done nothing at all compared to what you do. You should have said a heavy drinker and a bit of a bore.

CLIVE But you like him well enough. You don't mind him coming?

BETTY Anyone at all to break the monotony.

CLIVE But you have your mother. You have Ellen.

BETTY Ellen is a governess. My mother is my mother.

CLIVE I hoped when she came to visit she would be company for you.

BETTY I don't think mother is on a visit. I think she lives with us.

CLIVE I think she does.

BETTY Clive you are so good.

CLIVE But are you bored my love?

BETTY It's just that I miss you when you're away. We're not in this country to enjoy ourselves. If I lack society that is my form of service.

CLIVE That's a brave girl. So today has been all right? No fainting? No hysteria?

BETTY I have been very tranquil.

CLIVE Ah what a haven of peace to come home to. The coolth, the calm, the beauty.

BETTY There is one thing, Clive, if you don't mind.

CLIVE What can I do for you, my dear?

BETTY It's about Joshua.

CLIVE I wouldn't leave you alone here with a quiet mind if it weren't for Joshua.

BETTY Joshua doesn't like me.

CLIVE Joshua has been my boy for eight years. He has saved my life. I have saved his life. He is devoted to me and to mine. I have said this before.

BETTY He is rude to me. He doesn't do what I say. Speak to him.

CLIVE Tell me what happened.

BETTY He said something improper.

CLIVE Well, what?

BETTY I don't like to repeat it.

CLIVE I must insist.

BETTY I had left my book inside on the piano. I was in the hammock. I asked him to fetch it.

CLIVE And did he not fetch it?

BETTY Yes, he did eventually.

CLIVE And what did he say?

BETTY Clive—

CLIVE Betty.

BETTY He said Fetch it yourself. You've got legs under that dress.

CLIVE Joshua!

Joshua comes.

Joshua, madam says you spoke impolitely to her this afternoon.

JOSHUA Sir?

CLIVE When she asked you to pass her book from the piano.

JOSHUA She has the book, sir.

BETTY I have the book now, but when I told you—

CLIVE Betty, please, let me handle this. You didn't pass it at once?

JOSHUA No sir, I made a joke first.

CLIVE What was that?

JOSHUA I said my legs were tired, sir. That was funny because the book was very near, it would not make my legs tired to get it.

BETTY That's not true.

JOSHUA Did madam hear me wrong?

CLIVE She heard something else.

JOSHUA What was that, madam?

BETTY Never mind.

CLIVE Now Joshua, it won't do you know. Madam doesn't
like that kind of joke. You must do what madam says,
just do what she says and don't answer back. You know
your place, Joshua. I don't have to say any more.

JOSHUA No sir.

BETTY I expect an apology.

JOSHUA I apologise, madam.

CLIVE There now. It won't happen again, my dear. I'm
very shocked Joshua, very shocked.

Clive winks at Joshua, unseen by Betty.
Joshua goes.

CLIVE I think another drink, and send for the children,
and isn't that Harry riding down the hill? Wave, wave.
Just in time before dark. Cuts it fine, the blighter. Always a hothead, Harry.

BETTY Can he see us?

CLIVE Stand further forward. He'll see your white dress.
There, he waved back.

BETTY Do you think so? I wonder what he saw. Sometimes
sunset is so terrifying I can't bear to look.

CLIVE It makes me proud. Elsewhere in the empire the
sun is rising.

BETTY Harry looks so small on the hillside.

Ellen comes.

ELLEN Shall I bring the children?

BETTY Shall Ellen bring the children?

CLIVE Delightful.

BETTY Yes, Ellen, make sure they're warm. The night air is deceptive. Victoria was looking pale yesterday.

CLIVE My love.

Maud comes from inside the house.

MAUD Are you warm enough Betty?

BETTY Perfectly.

MAUD The night air is deceptive.

BETTY I'm quite warm. I'm too warm.

MAUD You're not getting a fever, I hope? She's not strong, you know, Clive. I don't know how long you'll keep her in this climate.

CLIVE I look after Her Majesty's domains, I think you can trust me to look after my wife.

Ellen comes carrying Victoria, age 2. Edward, aged 9, lags behind.

BETTY Victoria, my pet, say good evening to papa.

Clive takes Victoria on his knee.

CLIVE There's my sweet little Vicky. What have we done today?

BETTY She wore Ellen's hat.

CLIVE Did she wear Ellen's big hat like a lady? What a pretty.

BETTY And Joshua gave her a piggy back. Tell papa. Horsy with Joshy?

ELLEN She's tired.

CLIVE Nice Joshy played horsy. What a big strong Joshy. Did you have a gallop? Did you make him stop and go? Not very chatty tonight are we?

BETTY Edward, say good evening to papa.

CLIVE Edward my boy. Have you done your lessons well?

EDWARD Yes papa.

CLIVE Did you go riding?

EDWARD Yes papa.

CLIVE What's that you're holding?

BETTY It's Victoria's doll. What are you doing with it, Edward?

EDWARD Minding her.

BETTY Well I should give it to Ellen quickly. You don't want papa to see you with a doll.

CLIVE No, we had you with Victoria's doll once before, Edward.

ELLEN He's minding it for Vicky. He's not playing with it.

BETTY He's not playing with it, Clive. He's minding it for Vicky.

CLIVE Ellen minds Victoria, let Ellen mind the doll.

ELLEN Come, give it to me.

Ellen takes the doll.

EDWARD Don't pull her about. Vicky's very fond of her. She likes me to have her.

BETTY He's a very good brother.

CLIVE Yes, it's manly of you Edward, to take care of your little sister. We'll say no more about it. Tomorrow I'll take you riding with me and Harry Bagley. Would you like that?

EDWARD Is he here?

CLIVE He's just arrived. There Betty, take Victoria now. I must go and welcome Harry.

Clive tosses Victoria to Betty, who gives her to Ellen.

EDWARD Can I come, papa?

BETTY Is he warm enough?

EDWARD Am I warm enough?

CLIVE Never mind the women, Ned. Come and meet Harry.

They go. The women are left.
There is a silence.

MAUD I daresay Mr. Bagley will be out all day and we'll see nothing of him.

BETTY He plays the piano. Surely he will sometimes stay at home with us.

MAUD We can't expect it. The men have their duties and we have ours.

BETTY He won't have seen a piano for a year. He lives a very rough life.

ELLEN Will it be exciting for you, Betty?

MAUD Whatever do you mean, Ellen?

ELLEN We don't have very much society.

BETTY Clive is my society.

MAUD It's time Victoria went to bed.

ELLEN She'd like to stay up and see Mr. Bagley.

MAUD Mr. Bagley can see her tomorrow.

Ellen goes.

MAUD You let that girl forget her place, Betty.

BETTY Mother, she is governess to my son. I know what her place is. I think my friendship does her good. She is not very happy.

MAUD Young women are never happy.

BETTY Mother, what a thing to say.

MAUD Then when they're older they look back and see that comparatively speaking they were ecstatic.

BETTY I'm perfectly happy.

MAUD You are looking very pretty tonight. You were such a success as a young girl. You have made a most fortunate marriage. I'm sure you will be an excellent hostess to Mr. Bagley.

BETTY I feel quite nervous at the thought of entertaining.

MAUD I can always advise you if I'm asked.

BETTY What a long time they're taking. I always seem to be waiting for the men.

MAUD Betty you have to learn to be patient. I am patient. My mama was very patient.

Clive approaches, supporting Caroline Saunders.

CLIVE It is a pleasure. It is an honour. It is positively your duty to seek my help. I would be hurt, I would be insulted by any show of independence. Your husband would have been one of my dearest friends if he had lived. Betty, look who has come, Mrs. Saunders. She has ridden here all alone, amazing spirit. What will you have? Tea or something stronger? Let her lie down, she is overcome. Betty, you will know what to do.

Mrs. Saunders lies down.

MAUD I knew it. I heard drums. We'll be killed in our beds.

CLIVE Now, please, calm yourself.

MAUD I am perfectly calm. I am just outspoken. If it comes to being killed I shall take it as calmly as anyone.

CLIVE There is no cause for alarm. Mrs. Saunders has been alone since her husband died last year, amazing spirit. Not surprisingly, the strain has told. She has come to us as her nearest neighbours.

MAUD What happened to make her come?

CLIVE This is not an easy country for a woman.

MAUD Clive, I heard drums. We are not children.

CLIVE Of course you heard drums. The tribes are constantly at war, if the term is not too grand to grace their squabbles. Not unnaturally Mrs. Saunders would like the company of white women. The piano. Poetry.

BETTY We are not her nearest neighbours.

CLIVE We are among her nearest neighbours and I was a dear friend of her late husband. She knows that she will find a welcome here. She will not be disappointed. She will be cared for.

MAUD Of course we will care for her.

BETTY Victoria is in bed. I must go and say goodnight. Mother, please, you look after Mrs. Saunders.

CLIVE Harry will be here at once.

Betty goes.

MAUD How rash to go out after dark without a shawl.

CLIVE Amazing spirit. Drink this.

MRS. SAUNDERS Where am I?

MAUD You are quite safe.

MRS. SAUNDERS Clive? Clive? Thank God. This is very kind. How do you do? I am sorry to be a nuisance. Charmed. Have you a gun? I have a gun.

CLIVE There is no need for guns I hope. We are all friends here.

MRS. SAUNDERS I think I will lie down again.

Harry Bagley and Edward have approached.

MAUD Ah, here is Mr. Bagley.

EDWARD I gave his horse some water.

CLIVE You don't know Mrs. Saunders, do you Harry? She
has at present collapsed, but she is recovering thanks to
the good offices of my wife's mother who I think you've
met before. Betty will be along in a minute. Edward
will go home to school shortly. He is quite a young man
since you saw him.

HARRY I hardly knew him.

MAUD What news have you for us, Mr. Bagley?

CLIVE Do you know Mrs. Saunders, Harry? Amazing
spirit.

EDWARD Did you hardly know me?

HARRY Of course I knew you. I mean you have grown.

EDWARD What do you expect?

HARRY That's quite right, people don't get smaller.

MAUD Edward. You should be in bed.

EDWARD No, I'm not tired, I'm not tired am I Uncle
Harry?

HARRY I don't think he's tired.

CLIVE He is overtired. It is past his bedtime. Say goodnight.

EDWARD Goodnight, sir.

CLIVE And to your grandmother.

EDWARD Goodnight, grandmother.

Edward goes.

MAUD Shall I help Mrs. Saunders indoors? I'm afraid she may get a chill.

CLIVE Shall I give her an arm?

MAUD How kind of you Clive. I think I am strong enough.

Maud helps Mrs. Saunders into the house.

CLIVE Not a word to alarm the women.

HARRY Absolutely.

CLIVE I did some good today I think. Kept up some alliances. There's a lot of affection there.

HARRY They're affectionate people. They can be very cruel of course.

CLIVE Well they are savages.

HARRY Very beautiful people many of them.

CLIVE Joshua! *(to* HARRY*)* I think we should sleep with guns.

HARRY I haven't slept in a house for six months. It seems extremely safe.

Joshua comes.

CLIVE Joshua, you will have gathered there's a spot of bother. Rumours of this and that. You should be armed I think.

JOSHUA There are many bad men, sir. I pray about it. Jesus will protect us.

CLIVE He will indeed and I'll also get you a weapon. Betty, come and keep Harry company. Look in the barn, Joshua, every night.

Clive and Joshua go. Betty comes.

HARRY I wondered where you were.

BETTY I was singing lullabies.

HARRY When I think of you I always think of you with Edward in your lap.

BETTY Do you think of me sometimes then?

HARRY You have been thought of where no white woman has ever been thought of before.

BETTY It's one way of having adventures. I suppose I will never go in person.

HARRY That's up to you.

BETTY Of course it's not. I have duties.

HARRY Are you happy, Betty?

BETTY Where have you been?

HARRY Built a raft and went up the river. Stayed with some people. The king is always very good to me. They have a lot of skulls around the place but not white men's I think. I made up a poem one night. If I should die in this forsaken spot, There is a loving heart without a blot, Where I will live—and so on.

BETTY When I'm near you it's like going out into the jungle. It's like going up the river on a raft. It's like going out in the dark.

HARRY And you are safety and light and peace and home.

BETTY But I want to be dangerous.

HARRY Clive is my friend.

BETTY I am your friend.

HARRY I don't like dangerous women.

BETTY Is Mrs. Saunders dangerous?

HARRY Not to me. She's a bit of an old boot.
  Joshua comes, unobserved.

BETTY Am I dangerous?

HARRY You are rather.

BETTY Please like me.

HARRY I worship you.

BETTY Please want me.

HARRY I don't want to want you. Of course I want you.

BETTY What are we going to do?

HARRY I should have stayed on the river. The hell with it.
  He goes to take her in his arms, she runs away into the house. Harry stays where he is. He becomes aware of Joshua.

HARRY Who's there?

JOSHUA Only me sir.

HARRY Got a gun now have you?

JOSHUA Yes sir.

HARRY Where's Clive?

JOSHUA Going round the boundaries sir.

HARRY Have you checked there's nobody in the barns?

JOSHUA Yes sir.

HARRY Shall we go in a barn and fuck? It's not an order.

JOSHUA That's all right, yes.

They go off.

Scene 2

An open space some distance from the house. MRS. SAUNDERS *alone, breathless.* CLIVE *arrives.*

CLIVE Why? Why?

MRS. SAUNDERS Don't fuss, Clive, it makes you sweat.

CLIVE Why ride off now? Sweat, you would sweat if you were in love with somebody as disgustingly capricious as you are. You will be shot with poisoned arrows. You will miss the picnic. Somebody will notice I came after you.

MRS. SAUNDERS I didn't want you to come after me. I wanted to be alone.

CLIVE You will be raped by cannibals.

MRS. SAUNDERS I just wanted to get out of your house.

CLIVE My God, what women put us through. Cruel, cruel. I think you are the sort of woman who would enjoy whipping somebody. I've never met one before.

MRS. SAUNDERS Can I tell you something, Clive?

CLIVE Let me tell you something first. Since you came to the house I have had an erection twenty-four hours a day except for ten minutes after the time we had intercourse.

MRS. SAUNDERS I don't think that's physically possible.

CLIVE You are causing me appalling physical suffering. Is this the way to treat a benefactor?

MRS. SAUNDERS Clive, when I came to your house the other night I came because I was afraid. The cook was going to let his whole tribe in through the window.

CLIVE I know that, my poor sweet. Amazing—

MRS. SAUNDERS I came to you although you are not my nearest neighbour—

CLIVE Rather than to the old major of seventy-two.

MRS. SAUNDERS Because the last time he came to visit me I had to defend myself with a shotgun and I thought you would take no for an answer.

CLIVE But you've already answered yes.

MRS. SAUNDERS I answered yes once. Sometimes I want to say no.

CLIVE Women, my God. Look the picnic will start, I have to go to the picnic. Please Caroline—

MRS. SAUNDERS I think I will have to go back to my own house.

CLIVE Caroline, if you were shot with poisoned arrows do you know what I'd do? I'd fuck your dead body and poison myself. Caroline, you smell amazing. You terrify me. You are dark like this continent. Mysterious. Treacherous. When you rode to me through the night. When you fainted in my arms. When I came to you in your bed, when I lifted the mosquito netting, when I said let me in, let me in. Oh don't shut me out, Caroline, let me in.

He has been caressing her feet and legs. He disappears completely under her skirt.

MRS. SAUNDERS Please stop. I can't concentrate. I want to go home. I wish I didn't enjoy the sensation because I don't like you, Clive. I do like living in your house where there's plenty of guns. But I don't like you at all. But I do like the sensation. Well I'll have it then. I'll have it, I'll have it—

Voices are heard singing The First Noël.

Don't stop. Don't stop.

Clive comes out from under her skirt.

CLIVE The Christmas picnic. I came.

MRS. SAUNDERS I didn't.

CLIVE I'm all sticky.

MRS. SAUNDERS What about me? Wait.

CLIVE All right, are you? Come on. We mustn't be found.

MRS. SAUNDERS Don't go now.

CLIVE Caroline, you are so voracious. Do let go. Tidy yourself up. There's a hair in my mouth.

*Clive and Mrs. Saunders go off. Betty and Maud come,
with Joshua carrying hamper.*

MAUD I never would have thought a guinea fowl could
taste so like a turkey.

BETTY I had to explain to the cook three times.

MAUD You did very well dear.

*Joshua sits apart with gun. Edward and Harry with
Victoria on his shoulder, singing The First Noël. Maud
and Betty are unpacking the hamper. Clive arrives sep-
arately.*

MAUD This tablecloth was one of my mama's.

BETTY Uncle Harry playing horsy.

EDWARD Crackers crackers.

BETTY Not yet, Edward.

CLIVE And now the moment we have all been waiting for.

Clive opens champagne. General acclaim.

CLIVE Oh dear, stained my trousers, never mind.

EDWARD Can I have some?

MAUD Oh no Edward, not for you.

CLIVE Give him half a glass.

MAUD If your father says so.

CLIVE All rise please. To Her Majesty Queen Victoria, God
bless her, and her husband and all her dear children.

ALL The Queen.

EDWARD Crackers crackers.

*General cracker pulling, hats. Clive and Harry discuss
champagne.*

HARRY Excellent, Clive, wherever did you get it?

CLIVE I know a chap in French Equatorial Africa.

EDWARD I won, I won mama.

Ellen arrives.

BETTY Give a hat to Joshua, he'd like it.

*Edward takes hat to Joshua. Betty takes a ball from the
hamper and plays catch with Ellen. Murmurs of surprise and congratulations from the men whenever they
catch the ball.*

EDWARD Mama, don't play. You know you can't catch a
ball.

BETTY He's perfectly right. I can't throw either.

Betty sits down. Ellen has the ball.

EDWARD Ellen, don't you play either. You're no good. You
spoil it.

*Edward takes Victoria from Harry and gives her to El-
len. He takes the ball and throws it to Harry. Harry,
Clive and Edward play ball.*

BETTY Ellen come and sit with me. We'll be spectators
and clap.

Edward misses the ball.

CLIVE Butterfingers.

EDWARD I'm not.

HARRY Throw straight now.

EDWARD I did, I did.

CLIVE Keep your eye on the ball.

EDWARD You can't throw.

CLIVE Don't be a baby.

EDWARD I'm not, throw a hard one, throw a hard one—

CLIVE Butterfingers. What will Uncle Harry think of you?

EDWARD It's your fault. You can't throw. I hate you.
   He throws the ball wildly in the direction of Joshua.

CLIVE Now you've lost the ball. He's lost the ball.

EDWARD It's Joshua's fault. Joshua's butterfingers.

CLIVE I don't think I want to play any more. Joshua, find the ball will you?

EDWARD Yes, please play. I'll find the ball. Please play.

CLIVE You're so silly and you can't catch. You'll be no good at cricket.

MAUD Why don't we play hide and seek?

EDWARD Because it's a baby game.

BETTY You've hurt Edward's feelings.

CLIVE A boy has no business having feelings.

HARRY Hide and seek. I'll be it. Everybody must hide. This is the base, you have to get home to base.

EDWARD Hide and seek, hide and seek.

HARRY Can we persuade the ladies to join us?

MAUD I'm playing. I love games.

BETTY I always get found straight away.

ELLEN Come on, Betty, do. Vicky wants to play.

EDWARD You won't find me ever.

They all go except Clive, Harry, Joshua.

HARRY It is safe, I suppose?

CLIVE They won't go far. This is very much my territory and it's broad daylight. Joshua will keep an open eye.

HARRY Well I must give them a hundred. You don't know what this means to me Clive. A chap can only go on so long alone. I can climb mountains and go down rivers, but what's it for? For Christmas and England and games and women singing. This is the empire, Clive. It's not me putting a flag in new lands. It's you. The empire is one big family. I'm one of its black sheep, Clive. And I know you think my life is rather dashing. But I want you to know I admire you. This is the empire, Clive and I serve it. With all my heart.

CLIVE I think that's about a hundred.

HARRY Ready or not, here I come!

He goes.

CLIVE Harry Bagley is a fine man, Joshua. You should be proud to know him. He will be in history books.

JOSHUA Sir, while we are alone.

CLIVE Joshua of course, what is it? You always have my ear. Any time.

JOSHUA Sir, I have some information. The stable boys are not to be trusted. They whisper. They go out at night. They visit their people. Their people are not my people. I do not visit my people.

CLIVE Thank you, Joshua. They certainly look after Beauty. I'll be sorry to have to replace them.

JOSHUA They carry knives.

CLIVE Thank you, Joshua.

JOSHUA And, sir.

CLIVE I appreciate this, Joshua, very much.

JOSHUA Your wife.

CLIVE Ah, yes?

JOSHUA She also thinks Harry Bagley is a fine man.

CLIVE Thank you, Joshua.

JOSHUA Are you going to hide?

CLIVE Yes, yes I am. Thank you. Keep your eyes open Joshua.

JOSHUA I do, sir.

Clive goes. Joshua goes. Harry and Betty race back to base.

BETTY I can't run, I can't run at all.

HARRY There, I've caught you.

BETTY Harry, what are we going to do?

HARRY It's impossible, Betty.

BETTY Shall we run away together?

Maud comes.

MAUD I give up. Don't catch me. I have been stung.

HARRY Nothing serious I hope.

MAUD I have ointment in my bag. I always carry ointment. I shall just sit down and rest. I am too old for all this fun. Hadn't you better be seeking, Harry?

Harry goes. Maud and Betty are alone for some time. They don't speak. Harry and Edward race back.

EDWARD I won, I won, you didn't catch me.

HARRY Yes I did.

EDWARD Mama, who was first?

BETTY I wasn't watching. I think it was Harry.

EDWARD It wasn't Harry. You're no good at judging. I won, didn't I grandma?

MAUD I expect so, since it's Christmas.

EDWARD I won, Uncle Harry. I'm better than you.

BETTY Why don't you help Uncle Harry look for the others?

EDWARD Shall I?

HARRY Yes, of course.

BETTY Run along then. He's just coming.

Edward goes.

Harry, I shall scream.

HARRY Ready or not, here I come.

Harry runs off.

BETTY Why don't you go back to the house, mother, and rest your insect-bite?

MAUD Betty, my duty is here. I don't like what I see. Clive wouldn't like it, Betty. I am your mother.

BETTY Clive gives you a home because you are my mother.

Harry comes back.

HARRY I can't find anyone else. I'm getting quite hot.

BETTY Sit down a minute.

HARRY I can't do that. I'm he. How's your sting?

MAUD It seems to be swelling up.

BETTY Why don't you go home and rest? Joshua will go with you. Joshua!

HARRY I could take you back.

MAUD That would be charming.

BETTY You can't go. You're he.

Joshua comes.

BETTY Joshua, my mother wants to go back to the house. Will you go with her please.

JOSHUA Sir told me I have to keep an eye.

BETTY I am telling you to go back to the house. Then you can come back here and keep an eye.

MAUD Thank you Betty. I know we have our little differences, but I always want what is best for you.

Joshua and Maud go.

HARRY Don't give way. Keep calm.

BETTY I shall kill myself.

HARRY Betty, you are a star in my sky. Without you I would have no sense of direction. I need you, and I need you where you are, I need you to be Clive's wife. I need to go up rivers and know you are sitting here thinking of me.

BETTY I want more than that. Is that wicked of me?

HARRY Not wicked, Betty. Silly.

Edward calls in the distance.

EDWARD Uncle Harry, where are you?

BETTY Can't we ever be alone?

HARRY You are a mother. And a daughter. And a wife.

BETTY I think I shall go and hide again.

Betty goes. Harry goes. Clive chases Mrs. Saunders across the stage. Edward and Harry call in the distance.

EDWARD Uncle Harry!

HARRY Edward!

Edward comes.

EDWARD Uncle Harry!

Harry comes.

There you are. I haven't found anyone have you?

HARRY I wonder where they all are.

EDWARD Perhaps they're lost forever. Perhaps they're dead. There's trouble going on isn't there, and nobody says because of not frightening the women and children.

HARRY Yes, that's right.

EDWARD Do you think we'll be killed in our beds?

HARRY Not very likely.

EDWARD I can't sleep at night. Can you?

HARRY I'm not used to sleeping in a house.

EDWARD If I'm awake at night can I come and see you? I won't wake you up. I'll only come in if you're awake.

HARRY You should try to sleep.

EDWARD I don't mind being awake because I make up adventures. Once we were on a raft going down to the rapids. We've lost the paddles because we used them to fight off the crocodiles. A crocodile comes at me and I stab it again and again and the blood is everywhere and it tips up the raft and it has you by the leg and it's biting your leg right off and I take my knife and stab it in the throat and rip open its stomach and it lets go of you but it bites my hand but it's dead. And I drag you onto the river bank and I'm almost fainting with pain and we lie there in each other's arms.

HARRY Have I lost my leg?

EDWARD I forgot about the leg by then.

HARRY Hadn't we better look for the others?

EDWARD Wait. I've got something for you. It was in mama's box but she never wears it.

Edward gives Harry a necklace.

You don't have to wear it either but you might like it to look at.

HARRY It's beautiful. But you'll have to put it back.

EDWARD I wanted to give it to you.

HARRY You did. It can go back in the box. You still gave it to me. Come on now, we have to find the others.

EDWARD Harry, I love you.

HARRY Yes I know. I love you too.

EDWARD You know what we did when you were here before. I want to do it again. I think about it all the time. I try to do it to myself but it's not as good. Don't you want to any more?

HARRY I do, but it's a sin and a crime and it's also wrong.

EDWARD But we'll do it anyway won't we?

HARRY Yes of course.

EDWARD I wish the others would all be killed. Take it out now and let me see it.

HARRY No.

EDWARD Is it big now?

HARRY Yes.

EDWARD Let me touch it.

HARRY No.

EDWARD Just hold me.

HARRY When you can't sleep.

EDWARD We'd better find the others then. Come on.

HARRY Ready or not, here we come.

They go out with whoops and shouts. Betty and Ellen come.

BETTY Ellen, I don't want to play any more.

ELLEN Nor do I, Betty.

BETTY Come and sit here with me. Oh Ellen, what will become of me?

ELLEN Betty, are you crying? Are you laughing?

BETTY Tell me what you think of Harry Bagley.

ELLEN He's a very fine man.

BETTY No, Ellen, what you really think.

ELLEN I think you think he's very handsome.

BETTY And don't you think he is? Oh Ellen, you're so good and I'm so wicked.

ELLEN I'm not so good as you think.

Edward comes.

EDWARD I've found you.

ELLEN We're not hiding Edward.

EDWARD But I found you.

ELLEN We're not playing, Edward, now run along.

EDWARD Come on, Ellen, do play. Come on, mama.

ELLEN Edward, don't pull your mama like that.

BETTY Edward, you must do what your governess says. Go and play with Uncle Harry.

EDWARD Uncle Harry!

Edward goes.

BETTY Ellen, can you keep a secret?

ELLEN Oh yes, yes please.

BETTY I love Harry Bagley. I want to go away with him. There, I've said it, it's true.

ELLEN How do you know you love him?

BETTY I kissed him.

ELLEN Betty.

BETTY He held my hand like this. Oh I want him to do it again. I want him to stroke my hair.

ELLEN Your lovely hair. Like this, Betty?

BETTY I want him to put his arm around my waist.

ELLEN Like this, Betty?

BETTY Yes, oh I want him to kiss me again.

ELLEN Like this Betty?

Ellen kisses Betty.

BETTY Ellen, whatever are you doing? It's not a joke.

ELLEN I'm sorry, Betty. You're so pretty. Harry Bagley doesn't deserve you. You wouldn't really go away with him?

BETTY Oh Ellen, you don't know what I suffer. You don't know what love is. Everyone will hate me, but it's worth it for Harry's love.

ELLEN I don't hate you, Betty, I love you.

BETTY Harry says we shouldn't go away. But he says he worships me.

ELLEN I worship you Betty.

BETTY Oh Ellen, you are my only friend.

They embrace. The others have all gathered together. Maud has rejoined the party, and Joshua.

CLIVE Come along everyone, you mustn't miss Harry's conjuring trick.

Betty and Ellen go to join the others.

MAUD I didn't want to spoil the fun by not being here.

HARRY What is it that flies all over the world and is up my sleeve?

Harry produces a union jack from up his sleeve. General acclaim.

CLIVE I think we should have some singing now. Ladies, I rely on you to lead the way.

ELLEN We have a surprise for you. I have taught Joshua a Christmas carol. He has been singing it at the piano but I'm sure he can sing it unaccompanied, can't you, Joshua?

JOSHUA
   In the deep midwinter
   Frosty wind made moan,
   Earth stood hard as iron,
   Water like a stone.
   Snow had fallen snow on snow
   Snow on snow,
   In the deep midwinter
   Long long ago.

   What can I give him
   Poor as I am?
   If I were a shepherd
   I would bring a lamb.
   If I were a wise man
   I would do my part
   What I can I give him,
   Give my heart.

Scene 3

Inside the house. BETTY, MRS. SAUNDERS, MAUD *with* VICTORIA. *The blinds are down so the light isn't bright though it is day outside.* CLIVE *looks in.*

CLIVE Everything all right? Nothing to be frightened of.

Clive goes. Silence.

MAUD Clap hands, daddy comes, with his pockets full of plums. All for Vicky.

Silence.

MRS. SAUNDERS Who actually does the flogging?

MAUD I don't think we want to imagine.

MRS. SAUNDERS I imagine Joshua.

BETTY Yes I think it would be Joshua. Or would Clive do it himself?

MRS. SAUNDERS Well we can ask them afterwards.

MAUD I don't like the way you speak of it, Mrs. Saunders.

MRS. SAUNDERS How should I speak of it?

MAUD The men will do it in the proper way, whatever it is. We have our own part to play.

MRS. SAUNDERS Harry Bagley says they should just be sent away. I don't think he likes to see them beaten.

BETTY Harry is so tender-hearted. Perhaps he is right.

MAUD Harry Bagley is not altogether—He has lived in this country a long time without any responsibilities. It is part of his charm but it hasn't improved his judgment. If the boys were just sent away they would go back to the village and make more trouble.

MRS. SAUNDERS And what will they say about us in the village if they've been flogged?

BETTY Perhaps Clive should keep them here.

MRS. SAUNDERS That is never wise.

BETTY Whatever shall we do?

MAUD I don't think it is up to us to wonder. The men don't tell us what is going on among the tribes, so how can we possibly make a judgment?

MRS. SAUNDERS I know a little of what is going on.

BETTY Tell me what you know. Clive tells me nothing.

MAUD You would not want to be told about it, Betty. It is enough for you that Clive knows what is happening. Clive will know what to do. Your father always knew what to do.

BETTY Are you saying you would do something different, Caroline?

MRS. SAUNDERS I would do what I did at my own home. I left. I can't see any way out except to leave. I will leave here. I will keep leaving everywhere I suppose.

MAUD Luckily this household has a head. I am squeamish myself. But Clive is not.

BETTY You are leaving here then Caroline?

MRS. SAUNDERS Not immediately. I'm sorry.

Silence.

MRS. SAUNDERS I wonder if it's over.

Edward comes in.

BETTY Shouldn't you be with the men, Edward?

EDWARD I didn't want to see any more. They got what they deserved. Uncle Harry said I could come in.

MRS. SAUNDERS I never allowed the servants to be beaten in my own house. I'm going to find out what's happening.

Mrs. Saunders goes out.

BETTY Will she go and look?

MAUD Let Mrs. Saunders be a warning to you, Betty. She is alone in the world. You are not, thank God. Since your father died, I know what it is to be unprotected. Vicky is such a pretty little girl. Clap hands, daddy comes, with his pockets full of plums. All for Vicky.

Edward, meanwhile, has found the doll and is playing clap hands with her.

BETTY Edward, what have you got there?

EDWARD I'm minding her.

BETTY Edward, I've told you before, dolls are for girls.

MAUD Where is Ellen? She should be looking after Edward. *(She goes to the door)* Ellen! Betty, why do you let that girl mope about in her own room? That's not what she's come to Africa for.

BETTY You must never let the boys at school know you like dolls. Never, never. No one will talk to you, you won't be on the cricket team, you won't grow up to be a man like your papa.

EDWARD I don't want to be like papa. I hate papa.

MAUD Edward! Edward!

BETTY You're a horrid wicked boy and papa will beat you. Of course you don't hate him, you love him. Now give Victoria her doll at once.

EDWARD She's not Victoria's doll, she's my doll. She doesn't love Victoria and Victoria doesn't love her. Victoria never even plays with her.

MAUD Victoria will learn to play with her.

EDWARD She's mine and she loves me and she won't be happy if you take her away, she'll cry, she'll cry, she'll cry.

Betty takes the doll away, slaps him, bursts into tears. Ellen comes in.

BETTY Ellen, look what you've done. Edward's got the doll again. Now, Ellen, will you please do your job.

ELLEN Edward, you are a wicked boy. I am going to lock you in the nursery until supper time. Now go upstairs this minute.

She slaps Edward, who bursts into tears and goes out.

I do try to do what you want. I'm so sorry.

Ellen bursts into tears and goes out.

MAUD There now, Vicky's got her baby back. Where did Vicky's naughty baby go? Shall we smack her? Just a little smack? (MAUD *smacks the doll hard.*) There, now she's a good baby. Clap hands, daddy comes, with his pockets full of plums. All for Vicky's baby. When I was a child we honoured our parents. My mama was an angel.

Joshua comes in. He stands without speaking.

BETTY Joshua?

JOSHUA Madam?

BETTY Did you want something?

JOSHUA Sent to see the ladies are all right, madam.

Mrs. Saunders comes in.

MRS. SAUNDERS We're very well thank you Joshua, and how are you?

JOSHUA Very well thank you Mrs. Saunders.

MRS. SAUNDERS And the stable boys?

JOSHUA They have had justice, madam.

MRS. SAUNDERS So I saw. And does your arm ache?

MAUD This is not a proper conversation, Mrs. Saunders.

MRS. SAUNDERS You don't mind beating your own people?

JOSHUA Not my people, madam.

MRS. SAUNDERS A different tribe?

JOSHUA Bad people.

Harry and Clive come in.

CLIVE Well this is all very gloomy and solemn. Can we have the shutters open? The heat of the day has gone, we could have some light, I think. And cool drinks on the verandah, Joshua. Have some lemonade yourself. It is most refreshing.

Sunlight floods in as the shutters are opened. Edward comes.

EDWARD Papa, papa, Ellen tried to lock me in the nursery. Mama is going to tell you of me. I'd rather tell you myself. I was playing with Vicky's doll again and I know it's very bad of me. And I said I didn't want to be like you and I said I hated you. And it's not true and I'm sorry, I'm sorry and please beat me and forgive me.

CLIVE Well there's a brave boy to own up. You should always respect and love me, Edward, not for myself, I may not deserve it, but as I respected and loved my own father, because he was my father. Through our father we love our Queen and our God, Edward. Do you understand? It is something men understand.

EDWARD Yes papa.

CLIVE Then I forgive you and shake you by the hand. You spend too much time with the women. You may spend more time with me and Uncle Harry, little man.

EDWARD I don't like women. I don't like dolls. I love you, papa, and I love you, Uncle Harry.

CLIVE There's a fine fellow. Let us go out onto the verandah.

They all start to go. Edward takes Harry's hand and goes with him. Clive draws Betty back. They embrace.

BETTY Poor Clive.

CLIVE It was my duty to have them flogged. For you and Edward and Victoria, to keep you safe.

BETTY It is terrible to feel betrayed.

CLIVE You can tame a wild animal only so far. They revert to their true nature and savage your hand. Sometimes I feel the natives are the enemy. I know that is wrong. I know I have a responsibility towards them, to care for them and bring them all to be like Joshua. But there is something dangerous. Implacable. This whole continent is my enemy. I am pitching my whole mind and will and reason and spirit against it to tame it, and I sometimes feel it will break over me and swallow me up.

BETTY Clive, Clive, I am here. I have faith in you.

CLIVE Yes, I can show you my moments of weakness, Betty, because you are my wife and because I trust you. I trust you, Betty, and it would break my heart if you did not deserve that trust. Harry Bagley is my friend. It would break my heart if he did not deserve my trust.

BETTY I'm sorry, I'm sorry. Forgive me. It is not Harry's fault, it is all mine. Harry is noble. He has rejected me. It is my wickedness, I get bored, I get restless, I imagine things. There is something so wicked in me Clive.

CLIVE I have never thought of you having the weakness of your sex, only the good qualities.

BETTY I am bad, bad, bad—

CLIVE You are thoughtless, Betty, that's all. Women can be treacherous and evil. They are darker and more dangerous than men. The family protects us from that, you protect me from that. You are not that sort of woman. You are not unfaithful to me, Betty. I can't believe you are. It would hurt me so much to cast you off. That would be my duty.

BETTY No, no, no.

CLIVE Joshua has seen you kissing.

BETTY Forgive me.

CLIVE But I don't want to know about it. I don't want to know. I wonder of course, I wonder constantly. If Harry

Bagley was not my friend I would shoot him. If I shot
you every British man and woman would applaud me.
But no. It was a moment of passion such as women are
too weak to resist. But you must resist it, Betty, or it will
destroy us. We must fight against it. We must resist this
dark female lust, Betty, or it will swallow us up.

BETTY I do, I do resist. Help me. Forgive me.

CLIVE Yes I do forgive you. But I can't feel the same about
you as I did. You are still my wife and we still have duties
to the household.

*They go out arm in arm. As soon as they have gone
Edward sneaks back to get the doll, which has been
dropped on the floor. He picks it up and comforts it.
Joshua comes through with a tray of drinks.*

JOSHUA Baby. Sissy. Girly.

Joshua goes. Betty calls from off.

BETTY Edward?

Betty comes in.

BETTY There you are, my darling. Come, papa wants us all
to be together. Uncle Harry is going to tell how he
caught a crocodile. Mama's sorry she smacked you.

They embrace. Joshua comes in again, passing through.

BETTY Joshua, fetch me some blue thread from my sewing
box. It is on the piano.

JOSHUA You've got legs under that skirt.

BETTY Joshua.

JOSHUA And more than legs.

BETTY Edward, are you going to stand there and let a servant insult your mother?

EDWARD Joshua, get my mother's thread.

JOSHUA Oh little Eddy, playing at master. It's only a joke.

EDWARD Don't speak to my mother like that again.

JOSHUA Ladies have no sense of humour. You like a joke with Joshua.

EDWARD You fetch her sewing at once, do you hear me? You move when I speak to you, boy.

JOSHUA Yes sir, master Edward sir.

Joshua goes.

BETTY Edward, you were wonderful.

She goes to embrace him but he moves away.

EDWARD Don't touch me.

SONG—A Boy's Best Friend—ALL.

While plodding on our way, the toilsome road of life,
How few the friends that daily there we meet!
Not many will stand by in trouble and in strife,
With counsel and affection ever sweet!
But there is one whose smile will ever on us beam,
Whose love is dearer far than any other;
And wherever we may turn
This lesson we will learn
A boy's best friend is his mother.

Then cherish her with care
And smooth her silv'ry hair,
When gone you will never get another.
And wherever we may turn
This lesson we shall learn,
A boy's best friend is his Mother.

Scene 4

*The verandah as in Scene 1. Early morning. Nobody
there.* JOSHUA *comes out of the house slowly and stands
for some time doing nothing.* EDWARD *comes out.*

EDWARD Tell me another bad story, Joshua. Nobody else is
even awake yet.

JOSHUA First there was nothing and then there was the
great goddess. She was very large and she had golden
eyes and she made the stars and the sun and the earth.
But soon she was miserable and lonely and she cried
like a great waterfall and her tears made all the rivers in
the world. So the great spirit sent a terrible monster, a
tree with hundreds of eyes and a long green tongue,
and it came chasing after her and she jumped into a
lake and the tree jumped in after her, and she jumped
right up into the sky. And the tree couldn't follow, he
was stuck in the mud. So he picked up a big handful of
mud and he threw it at her, up among the stars, and it
hit her on the head. And she fell down onto the earth
into his arms and the ball of mud is the moon in the sky.
And then they had children which is all of us.

EDWARD It's not true, though.

JOSHUA Of course it's not true. It's a bad story. Adam and
Eve is true. God made man white like him and gave
him the bad woman who liked the snake and gave us all
this trouble.

Clive and Harry come out.

CLIVE Run along now, Edward. No, you may stay. You
mustn't repeat anything you hear to your mother or
your grandmother or Ellen.

EDWARD Or Mrs. Saunders?

CLIVE Mrs. Saunders is an unusual woman and does not require protection in the same way. Harry, there was trouble last night where we expected it. But it's all over now. Everything is under control but nobody should leave the house today I think.

HARRY Casualties?

CLIVE No, none of the soldiers hurt thank God. We did a certain amount, set a village on fire and so forth.

HARRY Was that necessary?

CLIVE Obviously, it was necessary, Harry, or it wouldn't have happened. The army will come and visit, no doubt. You'll like that, eh, Joshua, to see the British army? And a treat for you, Edward, to see the soldiers. Would you like to be a soldier?

EDWARD I'd rather be an explorer.

CLIVE Ah, Harry, like you, you see. I didn't know an explorer at his age. Breakfast, I think, Joshua.
   Clive and Joshua go in. Harry is following.

EDWARD Uncle.
   Harry stops.

EDWARD Harry, why won't you talk to me?

HARRY Of course I'll talk to you.

EDWARD If you won't be nice to me I'll tell father.

HARRY Edward, no, not a word, never, not to your mother, nobody, please. Edward, do you understand? Please.

EDWARD I won't tell. I promise I'll never tell. I've cut my finger and sworn.

HARRY There's no need to get so excited Edward. We can't be together all the time. I will have to leave soon anyway, and go back to the river.

EDWARD You can't, you can't go. Take me with you.

ELLEN Edward!

HARRY I have my duty to the Empire.

Harry goes in. Ellen comes out.

ELLEN Edward, breakfast time. Edward.

EDWARD I'm not hungry.

ELLEN Betty, please come and speak to Edward.

Betty comes.

BETTY Why what's the matter?

ELLEN He won't come in for breakfast.

BETTY Edward, I shall call your father.

EDWARD You can't make me eat.

He goes in. Betty is about to follow.

ELLEN Betty.

Betty stops.

ELLEN Betty, when Edward goes to school will I have to leave?

BETTY Never mind, Ellen dear, you'll get another place. I'll give you an excellent reference.

ELLEN I don't want another place, Betty. I want to stay with you forever.

BETTY If you go back to England you might get married, Ellen. You're quite pretty, you shouldn't despair of getting a husband.

ELLEN I don't want a husband. I want you.

BETTY Children of your own, Ellen, think.

ELLEN I don't want children, I don't like children. I just want to be alone with you, Betty, and sing for you and kiss you because I love you, Betty.

BETTY I love you too, Ellen dear. But women have their duty as soldiers have. You must be a mother if you can.

ELLEN Betty, Betty, I love you so much. I want to stay with you forever, my love for you is eternal, stronger than death. I'd rather die than leave you, Betty.

BETTY No you wouldn't. Ellen, don't be silly. Come, don't cry. You don't feel what you think you do. It's the loneliness here and the climate is very confusing. Come and have breakfast, Ellen dear, and I'll forget all about it.

Ellen goes, Clive comes.

BETTY Clive, please forgive me.

CLIVE Will you leave me alone?

Betty goes back into the house. Harry comes.

CLIVE Women, Harry. I envy you going into the jungle, a man's life.

HARRY I envy you.

CLIVE Harry, I know you do. I have spoken to Betty.

HARRY I assure you, Clive—

CLIVE Please say nothing about it.

HARRY My friendship for you—

CLIVE Absolutely. I know the friendship between us, Harry, is not something that could be spoiled by the weaker sex. Friendship between men is a fine thing. It is the noblest form of relationship.

HARRY I agree with you.

CLIVE There is the necessity of reproduction. The family is all important. And there is the pleasure. But what we put ourselves through to get that pleasure, Harry. When I heard about our fine fellows last night fighting those savages to protect us I thought yes, that is what I aspire to. I tell you Harry, in confidence, I suddenly got out of Mrs. Saunders' bed and came out here on the verandah and looked at the stars.

HARRY I couldn't sleep last night either.

CLIVE There is something dark about women, that threatens what is best in us. Between men that light burns brightly.

HARRY I didn't know you felt like that.

CLIVE Women are irrational, demanding, inconsistent, treacherous, lustful, and they smell different from us.

HARRY Clive—

CLIVE Think of the comradeship of men, Harry, sharing adventures, sharing danger, risking their lives together.

Harry takes hold of Clive.

CLIVE What are you doing?

HARRY Well, you said—

CLIVE I said what?

HARRY Between men.

Clive is speechless.

I'm sorry, I misunderstood, I would never have dreamt, I thought—

CLIVE My God, Harry, how disgusting.

HARRY You will not betray my confidence.

CLIVE I feel contaminated.

HARRY I struggle against it. You cannot imagine the shame. I have tried everything to save myself.

CLIVE The most revolting perversion. Rome fell, Harry, and this sin can destroy an empire.

HARRY It is not a sin, it is a disease.

CLIVE A disease more dangerous than diphtheria. Effeminacy is contagious. How I have been deceived. Your face does not look degenerate. Oh Harry, how did you sink to this?

HARRY Clive, help me, what am I to do?

CLIVE You have been away from England too long.

HARRY Where can I go except into the jungle to hide?

CLIVE You don't do it with the natives, Harry? My God, what a betrayal of the Queen.

HARRY Clive, I am like a man born crippled. Please help me.

CLIVE You must repent.

HARRY I have thought of killing myself.

CLIVE That is a sin too.

HARRY There is no way out. Clive I beg of you do not betray my confidence.

CLIVE I cannot keep a secret like this. Rivers will be named after you, it's unthinkable. You must save yourself from depravity. You must get married. You are not unattractive to women. What a relief that you and Betty were not after all—good God, how disgusting. Now Mrs. Saunders. She's a woman of spirit, she could go with you on your expeditions.

HARRY I suppose getting married wouldn't be any worse than killing myself.

CLIVE Mrs. Saunders! Mrs. Saunders! Ask her now, Harry. Think of England.

Mrs. Saunders comes.

Clive withdraws. Harry goes up to Mrs. Saunders.

HARRY Mrs. Saunders, will you marry me?

MRS. SAUNDERS Why?

HARRY We are both alone.

MRS. SAUNDERS I choose to be alone, Mr. Bagley. If I can look after myself, I'm sure you can. Clive, I have something important to tell you. I've just found Joshua putting earth on his head. He tells me his parents were killed last night by the British soldiers. I think you owe him an apology on behalf of the Queen.

CLIVE Joshua! Joshua!

MRS. SAUNDERS Mr. Bagley, I could never be a wife again. There is only one thing about marriage that I like.

Joshua comes.

CLIVE Joshua, I am horrified to hear what has happened. Good God!

MRS. SAUNDERS His father was shot. His mother died in the blaze.

Mrs. Saunders goes.

CLIVE Joshua, do you want a day off? Do you want to go to your people?

JOSHUA Not my people, sir.

CLIVE But you want to go to your parents' funeral?

JOSHUA No sir.

CLIVE Yes, Joshua, yes, your father and mother. I'm sure they were loyal to the crown. I'm sure it was all a terrible mistake.

JOSHUA My mother and father were bad people.

CLIVE Joshua, no.

JOSHUA You are my father and mother.

CLIVE Well really. I don't know what to say. That's very decent of you. Are you sure there's nothing I can do? You can have the day off you know.

Betty comes out followed by Edward.

BETTY What's the matter? What's happening?

CLIVE Something terrible has happened. No, I mean some relatives of Joshua's met with an accident.

JOSHUA May I go sir?

CLIVE Yes, yes of course. Good God, what a terrible thing. Bring us a drink will you Joshua?

Joshua goes.

EDWARD What? What?

BETTY Edward, go and do your lessons.

EDWARD What is it, Uncle Harry?

HARRY Go and do your lessons.

ELLEN Edward, come in here at once.

EDWARD What's happened, Uncle Harry?

Harry has moved aside, Edward follows him.
Ellen comes out.

HARRY Go away. Go inside. Ellen!

ELLEN Go inside, Edward. I shall tell your mother.

BETTY Go inside, Edward at once. I shall tell your father.

CLIVE Go inside, Edward. And Betty you go inside too.

Betty, Edward and Ellen go. Maud comes out.

CLIVE Go inside. And Ellen, you come outside.

Ellen comes out.

Mr. Bagley has something to say to you.

HARRY Ellen. I don't suppose you would marry me?

ELLEN What if I said yes?

CLIVE Run along now, you two want to be alone.

Harry and Ellen go out. Joshua brings Clive a drink.

JOSHUA The governess and your wife, sir.

CLIVE What's that, Joshua?

JOSHUA She talks of love to your wife, sir. I have seen them. Bad women.

CLIVE Joshua, you go too far. Get out of my sight.

Scene 5

The verandah. A table with a white cloth. A wedding cake and a large knife. Bottles and glasses. JOSHUA *is putting things on the table.* EDWARD *has the doll.* JOSHUA *sees him with it. He holds out his hand.* EDWARD *gives him the doll.* JOSHUA *takes the knife and cuts the doll open and shakes the sawdust out of it.* JOSHUA *throws the doll under the table.*

MAUD Come along Edward, this is such fun.

Everyone enters, triumphal arch for Harry and Ellen.

MAUD Your mama's wedding was a splendid occasion, Edward. I cried and cried.

Ellen and Betty go aside.

ELLEN Betty, what happens with a man? I don't know what to do.

BETTY You just keep still.

ELLEN And what does he do?

BETTY Harry will know what to do.

ELLEN And is it enjoyable?

BETTY Ellen, you're not getting married to enjoy yourself.

ELLEN Don't forget me, Betty.
  Ellen goes.

BETTY I think my necklace has been stolen Clive. I did so
  want to wear it at the wedding.

EDWARD It was Joshua. Joshua took it.

CLIVE Joshua?

EDWARD He did, he did, I saw him with it.

HARRY Edward, that's not true.

EDWARD It is, it is.

HARRY Edward, I'm afraid you took it yourself.

EDWARD I did not.

HARRY I have seen him with it.

CLIVE Edward, is that true? Where is it? Did you take your
  mother's necklace? And to try and blame Joshua, good
  God.
  Edward runs off.

BETTY Edward, come back. Have you got my necklace?

HARRY I should leave him alone. He'll bring it back.

BETTY I wanted to wear it. I wanted to look my best at your wedding.

HARRY You always look your best to me.

BETTY I shall get drunk.

Mrs. Saunders comes.

MRS. SAUNDERS The sale of my property is completed. I shall leave tomorrow.

CLIVE That's just as well. Whose protection will you seek this time?

MRS. SAUNDERS I shall go to England and buy a farm there. I shall introduce threshing machines.

CLIVE Amazing spirit.

He kisses her. Betty launches herself on Mrs. Saunders. They fall to the ground.

CLIVE Betty—Caroline—I don't deserve this—Harry, Harry.

Harry and Clive separate them. Harry holding Mrs. Saunders, Clive Betty.

CLIVE Mrs. Saunders, how can you abuse my hospitality? How dare you touch my wife? You must leave here at once.

BETTY Go away, go away. You are a wicked woman.

MAUD Mrs. Saunders, I am shocked. This is your hostess.

CLIVE Pack your bags and leave the house this instant.

MRS. SAUNDERS I was leaving anyway. There's no place for me here. I have made arrangements to leave tomorrow, and tomorrow is when I will leave. I wish you joy, Mr. Bagley.

Mrs. Saunders goes.

CLIVE No place for her anywhere I should think. Shocking behaviour.

BETTY Oh Clive, forgive me, and love me like you used to.

CLIVE Were you jealous my dove? My own dear wife!

MAUD Ah, Mr. Bagley, one flesh, you see.

Edward comes back with the necklace.

CLIVE Good God, Edward, it's true.

EDWARD I was minding it for mama because of the troubles.

CLIVE Well done, Edward, that was very manly of you. See Betty? Edward was protecting his mama's jewels from the rebels. What a hysterical fuss over nothing. Well done, little man. It is quite safe now. The bad men are dead. Edward, you may do up the necklace for mama.

Edward does up Betty's necklace, supervised by Clive, Joshua is drinking steadily. Ellen comes back.

MAUD Ah, here's the bride. Come along, Ellen, you don't cry at your own wedding, only at other people's.

CLIVE Now, speeches, speeches. Who is going to make a speech? Harry, make a speech.

HARRY I'm no speaker. You're the one for that.

ALL Speech, speech.

HARRY My dear friends—what can I say—the empire—
the family—the married state to which I have always
aspired—your shining example of domestic bliss—my
great good fortune in winning Ellen's love—happiest
day of my life.

Applause.

CLIVE Cut the cake, cut the cake.

*Harry and Ellen take the knife to cut the cake. Harry
steps on the doll under the table.*

HARRY What's this?

ELLEN Oh look.

BETTY Edward.

EDWARD It was Joshua. It was Joshua. I saw him.

CLIVE Don't tell lies again.

He hits Edward across the side of the head.

CLIVE Unaccustomed as I am to public speaking—

Cheers

Harry, my friend. So brave and strong and supple.
Ellen, from neath her veil so shyly peeking.
I wish you joy. A toast—the happy couple.
Dangers are past. Our enemies are killed.
—Put your arm round her, Harry, have a kiss—
All murmuring of discontent is stilled.
Long may you live in peace and joy and bliss.

*While he is speaking Joshua raises his gun to shoot
Clive. Only Edward sees. He does nothing to warn the
others. He puts his hands over his ears.*

BLACK.

ACT TWO

ACT II

Scene 1

Winter afternoon. Inside the hut of a one o'clock club, a children's playcentre in a park, VICTORIA *and* LIN, *mothers.* CATHY, LIN'*s daughter, age 4, played by a man, clinging to* LIN. VICTORIA *reading a book.*

CATHY Yum yum bubblegum.
　Stick it up your mother's bum
　When it's brown
　Pull it down
　Yum yum bubblegum.

LIN Like your shoes, Victoria.

CATHY Jack be nimble, Jack be quick
　Jack jump over the candlestick.
　Silly Jack, he should jump higher
　Goodness gracious, great balls of fire.

LIN Cathy, do stop. Do a painting.

CATHY You do a painting.

LIN You do a painting.

CATHY What shall I paint?

LIN Paint a house.

CATHY No.

LIN Princess.

CATHY No.

LIN Pirates.

CATHY Already done that.

LIN Spacemen.

CATHY I never paint spacemen. You know I never.

LIN Paint a car crash and blood everywhere.

CATHY No, don't tell me. I know what to paint.

LIN Go on then. You need an apron, where's an apron. Here.

CATHY Don't want an apron.

LIN Lift up your arms. There's a good girl.

CATHY I don't want to paint.

LIN Don't paint. Don't paint.

CATHY What shall I do? You paint. What shall I do mum?

VICTORIA There's nobody on the big bike, Cathy, quick.

Cathy goes out. Victoria is watching the children playing outside.

VICTORIA Tommy, it's Jimmy's gun. Let him have it. What the hell.

She goes on reading. She reads while she talks.

LIN I don't know how you can concentrate.

VICTORIA You have to or you never do anything.

LIN Yeh, well. It's really warm in here, that's one thing. It's better than standing out there. I got chilblains last winter.

VICTORIA It is warm.

LIN I suppose Tommy doesn't let you read much. I expect he talks to you while you're reading.

VICTORIA Yes, he does.

LIN I didn't get very far with that book you lent me.

VICTORIA That's all right.

LIN I was glad to have it, though. I sit with it on my lap while I'm watching the telly. Well, Cathy's off. She's frightened I'm going to leave her. It's the babyminder didn't work out when she was two, she still remembers. You can't get them used to other people if you're by yourself. It's no good blaming me. She clings round my knees every morning up the nursery and they don't say anything but they make you feel you're making her do it. But I'm desperate for her to go to school. I did cry when I left her the first day. You wouldn't, you're too fucking sensible. You'll call the teacher by her first name. I really fancy you.

VICTORIA What?

LIN Put your book down will you for five minutes. You didn't hear a word I said.

VICTORIA I don't get much time to myself.

LIN Do you ever go to the movies?

VICTORIA Tommy's very funny who he's left with. My mother babysits sometimes.

LIN Your husband could babysit.

VICTORIA But then we couldn't go to the movies.

LIN You could go to the movies with me.

VICTORIA Oh I see.

LIN Couldn't you?

VICTORIA Well yes, I could.

LIN Friday night?

VICTORIA What film are we talking about?

LIN Does it matter what film?

VICTORIA Of course it does.

LIN You choose then. Friday night.

Cathy comes in with gun, shoots them saying Kiou kiou kiou, and runs off again.

LIN Not in a foreign language, ok. You don't go to the movies to read.

Lin watches the children playing outside.

Don't hit him. Cathy, kill him. Point the gun, kiou, kiou, kiou. That's the way.

VICTORIA They've just banned war toys in Sweden.

LIN The kids'll just hit each other more.

VICTORIA Well psychologists do differ in their opinions as to whether or not aggression is innate.

LIN Yeh?

VICTORIA I'm afraid I do let Tommy play with guns and just hope he'll get it out of his system and not end up in the army.

LIN I've got a brother in the army.

VICTORIA Oh I'm sorry. Whereabouts is he stationed?

LIN Belfast.

VICTORIA Oh dear.

LIN I've got a friend who's Irish and we went on a Troops Out march. Now my dad won't speak to me.

VICTORIA I don't get on too well with my father either.

LIN And your husband? How do you get on with him?

VICTORIA Oh, fine. Up and down. You know. Very well. He helps with the washing up and everything.

LIN I left mine two years ago. He let me keep Cathy and I'm grateful for that.

VICTORIA You shouldn't be grateful.

LIN I'm a lesbian.

VICTORIA You still shouldn't be grateful.

LIN I'm grateful he didn't hit me harder than he did.

VICTORIA I suppose I'm very lucky with Martin.

LIN Don't get at me about how I bring up Cathy, ok?

VICTORIA I didn't.

LIN Yes you did. War toys. I'll give her a rifle for Christmas and blast Tommy's pretty head off for a start.

Victoria goes back to her book.

LIN I hate men.

VICTORIA You have to look at it in a historical perspective in terms of learnt behaviour since the industrial revolution.

LIN I just hate the bastards.

VICTORIA Well it's a point of view.

By now Cathy has come back in and started painting in many colours, without an apron. Edward comes in.

EDWARD Victoria, mother's in the park. She's walking round all the paths very fast.

VICTORIA By herself?

EDWARD I told her you were here.

VICTORIA Thanks.

EDWARD Come on.

VICTORIA Ten minutes talking to my mother and I have to spend two hours in a hot bath.

Victoria goes out.

LIN Shit, Cathy, what about an apron. I don't mind you having paint on your frock but if it doesn't wash off just don't tell me you can't wear your frock with paint on, ok?

CATHY Ok.

LIN You're gay, aren't you?

EDWARD I beg your pardon?

LIN I really fancy your sister. I thought you'd understand. You do but you can go on pretending you don't, I don't mind. That's lovely Cathy, I like the green bit.

EDWARD Don't go around saying that. I might lose my job.

LIN The last gardener was ever so straight. He used to flash at all the little girls.

EDWARD I wish you hadn't said that about me. It's not true.

LIN It's not true and I never said it and I never thought it and I never will think it again.

EDWARD Someone might have heard you.

LIN Shut up about it then.

Betty and Victoria come up.

BETTY It's quite a nasty bump.

VICTORIA He's not even crying.

BETTY I think that's very worrying. You and Edward always cried. Perhaps he's got concussion.

VICTORIA Of course he hasn't mummy.

BETTY That other little boy was very rough. Should you speak to somebody about him?

VICTORIA Tommy was hitting him with a spade.

BETTY Well he's a real little boy. And so brave not to cry. You must watch him for signs of drowsiness. And nausea. If he's sick in the night, phone an ambulance. Well, you're looking very well darling, a bit tired, a bit peaky. I think the fresh air agrees with Edward. He likes the open air life because of growing up in Africa. He misses the sunshine, don't you, darling? We'll soon have Edward back on his feet. What fun it is here.

VICTORIA This is Lin. And Cathy.

BETTY Oh Cathy what a lovely painting. What is it? Well I think it's a house on fire. I think all that red is a fire. Is that right? Or do I see legs, is it a horse? Can I have the lovely painting or is it for mummy? Children have such imagination, it makes them so exhausting. *(to* LIN*)* I'm sure you're wonderful, just like Victoria. I had help with my children. One does need help. That was in Africa of course so there wasn't the servant problem. This is my son Edward. This is—

EDWARD Lin.

BETTY Lin, this is Lin. Edward is doing something such fun, he's working in the park as a gardener. He does look exactly like a gardener.

EDWARD I am a gardener.

BETTY He's certainly making a stab at it. Well it will be a story to tell. I expect he will write a novel about it, or perhaps a television series. Well what a pretty child Cathy is. Victoria was a pretty child just like a little doll —you can't be certain how they'll grow up. I think

Victoria's very pretty but she doesn't make the most of herself, do you darling, it's not the fashion I'm told but there are still women who dress out of *Vogue*, well we hope that's not what Martin looks for, though in many ways I wish it was, I don't know what it is Martin looks for and nor does he I'm afraid poor Martin. Well I am rattling on. I like your skirt dear but your shoes won't do at all. Well do they have lady gardeners, Edward, because I'm going to leave your father and I think I might need to get a job, not a gardener really of course. I haven't got green fingers I'm afraid, everything I touch shrivels straight up. Vicky gave me a poinsettia last Christmas and the leaves all fell off on Boxing Day. Well good heavens, look what's happened to that lovely painting.

Cathy has slowly and carefully been going over the whole sheet with black paint. She has almost finished.

LIN What you do that for silly? It was nice.

CATHY I like your earrings.

VICTORIA Did you say you're leaving Daddy?

BETTY Do you darling? Shall I put them on you? My ears aren't pierced, I never wanted that, they just clip on the lobe.

LIN She'll get paint on you, mind.

BETTY There's a pretty girl. It doesn't hurt does it? Well you'll grow up to know you have to suffer a little bit for beauty.

CATHY Look mum I'm pretty, I'm pretty, I'm pretty.

LIN Stop showing off Cathy.

VICTORIA It's time we went home. Tommy, time to go home. Last go then, all right.

EDWARD Mum did I hear you right just now?

CATHY I want my ears pierced.

BETTY Ooh, not till you're big.

CATHY I know a girl got her ears pierced and she's three. She's got real gold.

BETTY I don't expect she's English, darling. Can I give her a sweety? I know they're not very good for the teeth, Vicky gets terribly cross with me. What does mummy say?

LIN Just one, thank you very much.

CATHY I like your beads.

BETTY Yes they are pretty. Here you are.

LIN *It is the necklace from ACT I.*

CATHY Look at me, look at me. Vicky, Vicky, Vicky look at me.

LIN You look lovely, come on now.

CATHY And your hat, and your hat.

LIN No, that's enough.

BETTY Of course she can have my hat.

CATHY Yes, yes, hat, hat.

CATHY Look look look.

LIN That's enough, please, stop it now. Hat off, bye bye hat.

CATHY Give me my hat.

LIN Bye bye beads.

BETTY It's just fun.

LIN It's very nice of you.

CATHY I want my beads.

LIN Where's the other earring?

CATHY I want my beads.

Cathy has the other earring in her hand. Meanwhile Victoria and Edward look for it.

EDWARD Is it on the floor?

VICTORIA Don't step on it.

EDWARD Where?

CATHY I want my beads. I want my beads.

LIN You'll have a smack.

Lin gets the earring from Cathy.

CATHY I want my beads.

BETTY Oh dear oh dear. Have you got the earring? Thank you darling.

CATHY I want my beads, you're horrid, I hate you, mum, you smell.

BETTY This is the point you see where one had help. Well it's been lovely seeing you dears and I'll be off again on my little walk.

VICTORIA You're leaving him? Really?

BETTY Yes you heard aright, Vicky, yes. I'm finding a little flat, that will be fun.

Betty goes.

Bye bye Tommy, granny's going now. Tommy don't hit that little girl, say goodbye to granny.

VICTORIA Fucking hell.

EDWARD Puking Jesus.

LIN That was news was it, leaving your father?

EDWARD They're going to want so much attention.

VICTORIA Does everybody hate their mothers?

EDWARD Mind you, I wouldn't live with him.

LIN Stop snivelling, pigface. Where's your coat? Be quiet now and we'll have doughnuts for tea and if you keep on we'll have dogshit on toast.

Cathy laughs so much she lies on the floor.

VICTORIA Tommy, you've had two last goes. Last last last last go.

LIN Not that funny, come on, coat on.

EDWARD Can I have your painting?

CATHY What for?

EDWARD For a friend of mine.

CATHY What's his name?

EDWARD Gerry.

CATHY How old is he?

EDWARD Thirty-two.

CATHY You can if you like. I don't care. Kiou kiou kiou kiou.

Cathy goes out. Edward takes the painting and goes out.

LIN Will you have sex with me?

VICTORIA I don't know what Martin would say. Does it count as adultery with a woman?

LIN You'd enjoy it.

Scene 2

Spring. Swing, bench, pond nearby. EDWARD *is gardening.* GERRY *sitting on a bench.*

EDWARD I sometimes pretend we don't know each other. And you've come to the park to eat your sandwiches and look at me.

GERRY That would be more interesting, yes. Come and sit down.

EDWARD If the superintendent comes I'll be in trouble. It's not my dinner time yet. Where were you last night? I think you owe me an explanation. We always do tell each other everything.

GERRY Is that a rule?

EDWARD It's what we agreed.

GERRY It's a habit we've got into. Look, I was drunk. I woke up at 4 o'clock on somebody's floor. I was sick. I hadn't any money for a cab. I went back to sleep.

EDWARD You could have phoned.

GERRY There wasn't a phone.

EDWARD Sorry.

GERRY There was a phone and I didn't phone you. Leave it alone, Eddy, I'm warning you.

EDWARD What are you going to do to me, then?

GERRY I'm going to the pub.

EDWARD I'll join you in ten minutes.

GERRY I didn't ask you to come. Two years I've been with Edward. You have to get away sometimes or you lose sight of yourself. The train from Victoria to Clapham still has those compartments without a corridor. As soon as I got on the platform I saw who I wanted. Slim hips, tense shoulders, trying not to look at anyone. I put my hand on my packet just long enough so that he couldn't miss it. The train came in. You don't want to get in too fast or some straight dumbo might get in with you. I sat by the window. I couldn't see where the fuck he'd got to. Then just as the whistle went he got in. Great. It's a six-minute journey so you can't start anything you can't finish. I stared at him and he unzipped his flies. Then he stopped. So I stood up and took my cock out. He took me in his mouth and shut his eyes tight. He was sort of mumbling it about as if he wasn't sure what to do, so I said, 'A bit tighter son' and he said 'Sorry' and then got on with it. He was jerking off with his left hand, and I could see he'd got a fairsized one. I wished he'd keep still so I could see his watch. I was getting really turned on. What if we pulled into Clapham Junction now. Of course by the time we sat down again the train was just slowing up. I felt wonderful. Then he started talking. It's better if nothing is said. Once you find he's a librarian in Walthamstow with a special interest in science fiction and lives with his aunt, then forget it. He said I hope you don't think I do this all the time. I said I hope you will from now on. He said he would if I was on the train, but why don't we go out for a meal? I opened the door before the train stopped. I told him I live with somebody, I don't want to know. He was jogging sideways to keep up. He said what's your phone number, you're my ideal physical type, what sign of the zodiac are you? Where do you live? Where are you going now? It's not fair. I saw him at Victoria a couple of months later and I went straight down to the end of the platform and I picked up somebody really great who never said a word, just smiled.

Cathy is on the swing.

CATHY Batman and Robin
  Had a batmobile
  Robin done a fart
  And paralysed the wheel
  The wheel couldn't take it
  The engine fell apart
  All because of Robin
  And his supersonic fart

Cathy goes. Martin, Victoria and Betty walking slowly.

MARTIN Tom!

BETTY He'll fall in.

VICTORIA No he won't.

MARTIN Don't go too near the edge Tom. Throw the bread from there. The ducks can get it.

BETTY I'll never be able to manage. If I can't even walk down the street by myself. Everything looks so fierce.

VICTORIA Just watch Tommy feeding the ducks.

BETTY He's going to fall in. Make Martin make him move back.

VICTORIA He's not going to fall in.

BETTY It's since I left your father.

VICTORIA Mummy, it really was the right decision.

BETTY Everything comes at me from all directions. Martin despises me.

VICTORIA Of course he doesn't, mummy.

BETTY Of course he does.

MARTIN Throw the bread. That's the way. The duck can get it. Quack quack quack quack quack.

BETTY I don't want to take pills. Lin says you can't trust doctors.

VICTORIA You're not taking pills. You're doing very well.

BETTY But I'm so frightened.

VICTORIA What are you frightened of?

BETTY Victoria, you always ask that as if there was suddenly going to be an answer.

VICTORIA Are you all right sitting there?

BETTY Yes, yes. Go and be with Martin.

Victoria joins Martin, Betty stays sitting on the bench.

MARTIN You take the job, you go to Manchester. You turn it down, you stay in London. People are making decisions like this every day of the week. It needn't be for more than a year. You get long vacations. Our relationship might well stand the strain of that, and if it doesn't we're better out of it. I don't want to put any pressure on you. I'd just like to know so we can sell the house. I think we're moving into an entirely different way of life if you go to Manchester because it won't end there. We could keep the house as security for Tommy but he might as well get used to the fact that life nowadays is insecure. You should ask your mother what she thinks and then do the opposite. I could just take that room in Barbara's house, and then we could babysit for each other. You think that means I want to fuck Barbara. I don't. Well, I do, but I won't. And even if I did, what's a fuck between friends? What are we meant to do it with, strangers? Whatever you want to do, I'll be delighted. If you could just let me know what it is I'm to be delighted about. Don't cry again, Vicky, I'm not the sort of man who makes women cry.

Lin has come in and sat down with Betty, Cathy joins them. She is wearing a pink dress and carrying a rifle.

LIN I've bought her three new frocks. She won't wear jeans to school any more because Tracy and Mandy called her a boy.

CATHY Tracy's got a perm.

LIN You should have shot them.

CATHY They're coming to tea and we've got to have trifle. Not trifle you make, trifle out of a packet. And you've got to wear a skirt. And tights.

LIN Tracy's mum wears jeans.

CATHY She does not. She wears velvet.

BETTY Well I think you look very pretty. And if that gun has caps in it please take it a long way away.

CATHY It's got red caps. They're louder.

MARTIN Do you think you're well enough to do this job? You don't have to do it. No one's going to think any the less of you if you stay here with me. There's no point being so liberated you make yourself cry all the time. You stay and we'll get everything sorted out. What it is about sex, when we talk while it's happening I get to feel it's like a driving lesson. Left, right, a little faster, carry on, slow down—

Cathy shoots Victoria.

CATHY You're dead Vicky.

VICTORIA Aaaargh.

CATHY Fall over.

VICTORIA I'm not falling over, the ground's wet.

CATHY You're dead.

VICTORIA Yes, I'm dead.

CATHY The Dead Hand Gang fall over. They said I had to fall over in the mud or I can't play. That duck's a mandarin.

MARTIN Which one? Look, Tommy.

CATHY That's a diver. It's got a yellow eye and it dives. That's a goose. Tommy doesn't know it's a goose, he thinks it's a duck. The babies get eaten by weasels. Kiou kiou.

Cathy goes.

MARTIN So I lost my erection last night not because I'm not prepared to talk, it's just that taking in technical information in a different part of the brain and also I don't like to feel that you do it better to yourself. I have read the Hite report. I do know that women have to learn to get their pleasure despite our clumsy attempts at expressing undying devotion and ecstasy, and that what we spent our adolescence thinking was an animal urge we had to suppress is in fact a fine art we have to acquire. I'm not like whatever percentage of American men have become impotent as a direct result of women's liberation, which I am totally in favour of, more I sometimes think than you are yourself. Nor am I one of your villains who sticks it in, bangs away, and falls asleep. My one aim is to give you pleasure. My one aim is to give you rolling orgasms like I do other women. So why the hell don't you have them? My analysis for what it's worth is that despite all my efforts you still feel dominated by me. I in fact think it's very sad that you don't feel able to take that job. It makes me feel very guilty. I don't want you to do it just because I encourage you to do it. But don't you think you'd feel better if you did take the job? You're the one who's talked about freedom. You're the one who's experimenting with bi-sexuality, and I don't stop you, I think women have something to give each other. You seem to need the mutual support. You find me too overwhelming. So follow it through, go away, leave me and Tommy alone for a bit, we can manage perfectly well without you. I'm not putting any pressure on you but I don't think you're

being a whole person. God knows I do everything I can
to make you stand on your own two feet. Just be yourself. You don't seem to realise how insulting it is to me
that you can't get yourself together.

Martin and Vic go.

BETTY You must be very lonely yourself with no husband.
You don't miss him?

LIN Not really, no.

BETTY Maybe you like being on your own.

LIN I'm seeing quite a lot of Vicky. I don't live alone. I live
with Cathy.

BETTY I would have been frightened when I was your age.
I thought, the poor children, their mother all alone.

LIN I've a lot of friends.

BETTY I find when I'm making tea I put out two cups. It's
strange not having a man in the house. You don't know
who to do things for.

LIN Yourself.

BETTY Oh, that's very selfish.

LIN Have you any women friends?

BETTY I've never been so short of men's company that
I've had to bother with women.

LIN Don't you like women?

BETTY They don't have such interesting conversations as
men. There has never been a woman composer of ge-
nius. They don't have a sense of humour. They spoil

things for themselves with their emotions. I can't say I do like women very much, no.

LIN But you're a woman.

BETTY There's nothing says you have to like yourself.

LIN Do you like me?

BETTY There's no need to take it personally, Lin.

Martin and Vic come back.

MARTIN Did you know if you put cocaine on your prick you can keep it up all night? The only thing is of course it goes numb so you don't feel anything. But you would, that's the main thing. I just want to make you happy.

BETTY Vicky I'd like to go home.

VICTORIA Yes, mummy, of course.

BETTY I'm sorry dear.

VICTORIA I think Tommy would like to stay out a bit longer.

LIN Hello, Martin. We do keep out of each other's way.

MARTIN I think that's the best thing to do.

BETTY Perhaps you'd walk home with me, Martin. I do feel safer with a man. The park is so large the grass seems to tilt.

MARTIN Yes, I'd like to go home and do some work. I'm writing a novel about women from the women's point of view.

Martin and Betty go. Lin and Victoria are alone. They embrace.

VICTORIA Why the hell can't he just be a wife and come with me? Why does Martin make me tie myself in knots? No wonder we can't just have a simple fuck. No, not Martin, why do I make myself tie myself in knots. It's got to stop, Lin. I'm not like that with you. Would you love me if I went to Manchester?

LIN Yes.

VICTORIA Would you love me if I went on a climbing expedition in the Andes mountains?

LIN Yes.

VICTORIA Would you love me if my teeth fell out?

LIN Yes.

VICTORIA Would you love me if I loved ten other people?

LIN And me?

VICTORIA Yes.

LIN Yes.

VICTORIA And I feel apologetic for not being quite so subordinate as I was. I am more intelligent than him. I am brilliant.

LIN Leave him Vic. Come and live with me.

VICTORIA Don't be silly.

LIN Silly, Christ, don't then. I'm not asking because I need to live with someone. I'd enjoy it, that's all, we'd both enjoy it. Fuck you. Cathy, for fuck's sake stop throwing stones at the ducks. The man's going to get you.

VICTORIA What man? Do you need a man to frighten your child with?

LIN My mother said it.

VICTORIA You're so inconsistent, Lin.

LIN I've changed who I sleep with, I can't change everything.

VICTORIA Like when I had to stop you getting a job in a boutique and collaborating with sexist consumerism.

LIN I should have got that job, Cathy would have liked it. Why shouldn't I have some decent clothes? I'm sick of dressing like a boy, why can't I look sexy, wouldn't you love me?

VICTORIA Lin, you've no analysis.

LIN No but I'm good at kissing aren't I? I give Cathy guns, my mum didn't give me guns. I dress her in jeans, she wants to wear dresses. I don't know. I can't work it out, I don't want to. You read too many books, you get at me all the time, you're worse to me than Martin is to you, you piss me off, my brother's been killed, I'm sorry to win the argument that way but there it is.

VICTORIA What do you mean win the argument?

LIN I mean be nice to me.

VICTORIA In Belfast?

LIN I heard this morning. Don't don't start. I've hardly seen him for two years. I rung my father. You'd think I'd shot him myself. He doesn't want me to go to the funeral.

Cathy approaches.

VICTORIA What will you do?

LIN Go of course.

CATHY What is it? Who's killed? What?

LIN It's Bill. Your uncle. In the army. Bill that gave you the blue teddy.

CATHY Can I have his gun?

LIN It's time we went home. Time you went to bed.

CATHY No it's not.

LIN We go home and you have tea and you have a bath and you go to bed.

CATHY Fuck off.

LIN Cathy shut up.

VICTORIA It's only half past five, why don't we—

LIN I'll tell you why she has to go to bed—

VICTORIA She can come home with me.

LIN Because I want her out of the fucking way.

VICTORIA She can come home with me.

CATHY I'm not going to bed.

LIN I want her home with me not home with you, I want her in bed, I want today over.

CATHY I'm not going to bed.

Lin hits Cathy, Cathy cries.

LIN And shut up or I'll give you something to cry for.

CATHY I'm not going to bed.

VICTORIA Cathy—

LIN You keep out of it.

VICTORIA Lin for God's sake.

They are all shouting. Cathy runs off. Lin and Victoria are silent. Then they laugh and embrace.

LIN Where's Tommy?

VICTORIA What? Didn't he go with Martin?

LIN Did he?

VICTORIA God oh God.

LIN Cathy! Cathy!

VICTORIA I haven't thought about him. How could I not think about him? Tommy!

LIN Cathy! Come on, quick, I want some help.

VICTORIA Tommy! Tommy!

Cathy comes back.

LIN Where's Tommy? Have you seen him? Did he go with Martin? Do you know where he is?

CATHY I showed him the goose. We went in the bushes.

LIN Then what?

CATHY I came back on the swing.

VICTORIA And Tommy? Where was Tommy?

CATHY He fed the ducks.

LIN No that was before.

CATHY He did a pee in the bushes. I helped him with his trousers.

VICTORIA And after that?

CATHY He fed the ducks.

VICTORIA No no.

CATHY He liked the ducks. I expect he fell in.

LIN Did you see him fall in?

VICTORIA Tommy! Tommy!

LIN What's the last time you saw him?

CATHY He did a pee.

VICTORIA Mummy said he would fall in. Oh God, Tommy!

LIN We'll go round the pond. We'll go opposite ways round the pond.

ALL *(Shout)* Tommy!

Victoria and Lin go off opposite sides. Cathy goes on the swing, standing up.

CATHY Georgy Best superstar
Walks like a woman and wears a bra.
There he is! I see him! Mum! Vicky! There he is! He's in
the bushes.

Lin comes back.

LIN Come on Cathy love, let's go home.

CATHY Vicky's got him.

LIN Come on.

CATHY Is she cross?

LIN No. Come on.

CATHY I found him.

LIN Yes. Come on.

Cathy gets off the bench. Cathy and Lin hug.

CATHY I'm watching telly.

LIN Ok.

CATHY After the news.

LIN Ok.

CATHY I'm not going to bed.

LIN Yes you are.

CATHY I'm not going to bed now.

LIN Not now but early.

CATHY How early?

LIN Not late.

CATHY How not late?

LIN Early.

CATHY How early?

LIN Not late.

They go off together. Gerry comes on. He waits. Edward comes. He has changed out of his work clothes.

EDWARD I've got some fish for dinner. I thought I'd make a cheese sauce.

GERRY I won't be in.

EDWARD Where are you going?

GERRY For a start I'm going to a sauna. Then I'll see.

EDWARD All right. What time will you be back? We'll eat then.

GERRY You're getting like a wife.

EDWARD I don't mind that.

GERRY Why don't I do the cooking sometime?

EDWARD You can if you like. You're just not so good at it that's all. Do it tonight.

GERRY I won't be in tonight.

EDWARD Do it tomorrow. If we can't eat it we can always go to a restaurant.

GERRY Stop it.

EDWARD Stop what?

GERRY Just be yourself.

EDWARD I don't know what you mean. Everyone's always tried to stop me being feminine and now you are too.

GERRY You're putting it on.

EDWARD I like doing the cooking. I like being fucked. You do like me like this really.

GERRY I'm bored Eddy.

EDWARD Go to the sauna.

GERRY And you'll stay home and wait up for me.

EDWARD No, I'll go to bed and read a book.

GERRY Or knit. You could knit me a pair of socks.

EDWARD I might knit. I like knitting.

GERRY I don't mind if you knit. I don't want to be married.

EDWARD I do.

GERRY Well I'm divorcing you.

EDWARD I wouldn't want to keep a man who wants his freedom.

GERRY Eddy, do stop playing the injured wife, it's not funny.

EDWARD I'm not playing. It's true.

GERRY I'm not the husband so you can't be the wife.

EDWARD I'll always be here, Gerry, if you want to come back. I know you men like to go off by yourselves. I don't think I could love deeply more than once. But I don't think I can face life on my own so don't leave it too long or it may be too late.

GERRY What are you trying to turn me into?

EDWARD A monster, darling, which is what you are.

GERRY I'll collect my stuff from the flat in the morning.

Gerry goes. Edward sits on the bench. It gets darker. Victoria comes.

VICTORIA Tommy dropped a toy car somewhere, you haven't seen it? It's red. He says it's his best one. Oh the hell with it. Martin's reading him a story. There, isn't it quiet?

They sit on the bench, holding hands.

EDWARD I like women.

VICTORIA That should please mother.

EDWARD No listen Vicky. I'd rather be a woman. I wish I had breasts like that, I think they're beautiful. Can I touch them?

VICTORIA What, pretending they're yours?

EDWARD No, I know it's you.

VICTORIA I think I should warn you I'm enjoying this.

EDWARD I'm sick of men.

VICTORIA I'm sick of men.

EDWARD I think I'm a lesbian.

Scene 3

The park. Summer night. VICTORIA, LIN *and* EDWARD *drunk.*

LIN Where are you?

VICTORIA Come on.

EDWARD Do we sit in a circle?

VICTORIA Sit in a triangle.

EDWARD You're good at mathematics. She's good at mathematics.

VICTORIA Give me your hand. We all hold hands.

EDWARD Do you know what to do?

LIN She's making it up.

VICTORIA We start off by being quiet.

EDWARD What?

LIN Hush.

EDWARD Will something appear?

VICTORIA It was your idea.

EDWARD It wasn't my idea. It was your book.

LIN You said call up the goddess.

EDWARD I don't remember saying that.

LIN We could have called her on the telephone.

EDWARD Don't be so silly, this is meant to be frightening.

LIN Kiss me.

VICTORIA Are we going to do it?

LIN We're doing it.

VICTORIA A ceremony.

LIN It's very sexy, you said it is. You said the women were priests in the temples and fucked all the time. I'm just helping.

VICTORIA As long as it's sacred.

LIN It's very sacred.

VICTORIA Innin, Innana, Nana, Nut, Anat, Anahita, Istar, Isis.

LIN I can't remember all that.

VICTORIA Lin! Innin, Innana, Nana, Nut, Anat, Anahita, Istar, Isis.

Lin and Edward join in and continue the chant under Victoria's speech.

Goddess of many names, oldest of the old, who walked in chaos and created life, hear us calling you back through time, before Jehovah, before Christ, before men drove you out and burnt your temples, hear us, Lady, give us back what we were, give us the history we haven't had, make us the women we can't be.

ALL Innin, Innana, Nana, Nut, Anat, Anahita, Istar, Isis.

Chant continues under other speeches.

LIN Come back, goddess.

VICTORIA Goddess of the sun and the moon her brother, little goddess of Crete with snakes in your hands.

LIN Goddess of breasts.

VICTORIA Goddess of cunts.

LIN Goddess of fat bellies and babies. And blood blood blood.

Chant continues.

LIN I see her.

EDWARD What?

They stop chanting.

LIN I see her. Very tall. Snakes in her hands. Light light light—look out! Did I give you a fright?

EDWARD I was terrified.

VICTORIA Don't spoil it Lin.

LIN It's all out of a book.

VICTORIA Innin Innana—I can't do it now. I was really enjoying myself.

LIN She won't appear with a man here.

VICTORIA They had men, they had sons and lovers.

EDWARD They had eunuchs.

LIN Don't give us ideas.

VICTORIA There's Attis and Tammuz, they're torn to pieces.

EDWARD Tear me to pieces, Lin.

VICTORIA The priestess chose a lover for a year and he was king because she chose him and then he was killed at the end of the year.

EDWARD Hurray.

VICTORIA And the women had the children and nobody knew it was done by fucking so they didn't know about fathers and nobody cared who the father was and the property was passed down through the maternal line—

LIN Don't turn it into a lecture, Vicky, it's meant to be an orgy.

VICTORIA It never hurts to understand the theoretical background. You can't separate fucking and economics.

LIN Give us a kiss.

EDWARD Shut up, listen.

LIN What?

EDWARD There's somebody there.

LIN Where?

EDWARD There.

VICTORIA The priestesses used to make love to total strangers.

LIN Go on then, I dare you.

EDWARD Go on, Vicky.

VICTORIA He won't know it's a sacred rite in honour of the goddess.

EDWARD We'll know.

LIN We can tell him.

EDWARD It's not what he thinks, it's what we think.

LIN Don't tell him till after, he'll run a mile.

VICTORIA Hello. We're having an orgy. Do you want me to suck your cock?

The stranger approaches. It is Martin.

MARTIN There you are. I've been looking everywhere. What the hell are you doing? Do you know what the time is? You're all pissed out of your minds.

They leap on Martin, pull him down and start to make love to him.

MARTIN Well that's all right. If all we're talking about is having a lot of sex there's no problem. I was all for the sixties when liberation just meant fucking.

Another stranger approaches.

LIN Hey you, come here. Come and have sex with us.

VICTORIA Who is it?

The stranger is a soldier.

LIN It's my brother.

EDWARD Lin, don't.

LIN It's my brother.

VICTORIA It's her sense of humour, you get used to it.

LIN Shut up Vicky, it's my brother. Isn't it? Bill?

SOLDIER Yes it's me.

LIN And you are dead.

SOLDIER Fucking dead all right yeh.

LIN Have you come back to tell us something?

SOLDIER No I've come for a fuck. That was the worst thing in the fucking army. Never fucking let out. Can't fucking talk to Irish girls. Fucking bored out of my fucking head. That or shit scared. For five minutes I'd be glad I wasn't bored, then I was fucking scared. Then we'd come in and I'd be glad I wasn't scared and then I was fucking bored. Spent the day reading fucking porn and the fucking night wanking. Man's fucking life in the fucking army? No fun when the fucking kids hate you. I got so I fucking wanted to kill someone and I got fucking killed myself and I want a fuck.

LIN I miss you. Bill. Bill.

Lin collapses. Soldier goes. Victoria comforts Lin.

EDWARD Let's go home.

LIN Victoria, come home with us. Victoria's coming to live with me and Edward.

MARTIN Tell me about it in the morning.

LIN It's true.

VICTORIA It is true.

MARTIN Tell me when you're sober.

Edward, Lin, Victoria go off together. Martin goes off alone. Gerry comes on.

GERRY I come here sometimes at night and pick somebody up. Sometimes I come here at night and don't pick anybody up. I do also enjoy walking about at night. There's never any trouble finding someone. I can have sex any time. You might not find the type you most fancy every day of the week, but there's plenty of people about who just enjoy having a good time. I quite like living alone. If I live with someone I get annoyed with them. Edward always put on Capital radio when he got up. The silence gets wasted. I wake up at four o'clock sometimes. Birds. Silence. If I bring somebody home I never let them stay the night. Edward! Edward!

Edward from Act 1 comes on.

EDWARD Gerry I love you.

GERRY Yes, I know. I love you, too.

EDWARD You know what we did? I want to do it again. I think about it all the time. Don't you want to any more?

GERRY Yes, of course.

SONG Cloud Nine

It'll be fine when you reach Cloud 9.

Mist was rising and the night was dark
Me and my baby took a walk in the park
He said Be mine and you're on Cloud 9.

Better watch out when you're on Cloud 9.

Smoked some dope on the playground swings
Higher and higher on true love's wings
He said Be mine and you're on Cloud 9.

Twentyfive years on the same Cloud 9.

Who did she meet on her first blind date?
The guys were no surprise but the lady was great
They were women in love, they were on Cloud 9.

Two the same, they were on Cloud 9.

The bride was sixtyfive, the groom was seventeen,
They fucked in the back of the black limousine.
It was divine in their silver Cloud 9.

Simply divine in their silver Cloud 9.

The wife's lover's children and my lover's wife,
Cooking in my kitchen, confusing my life.
And it's upside down when you reach Cloud 9.

Upside down when you reach Cloud 9.

Scene 4

The park. Afternoon in late summer. MARTIN,
CATHY, EDWARD.

CATHY Under the bramble bushes
   Under the sea boom boom boom
   True love for you my darling
   True love for me my darling
   When we are married
   We'll raise a family
   Boy for you, girl for me,
   Boom tiddley oom boom.
   SEXY

EDWARD You'll have Tommy and Cathy tonight then ok?
   Tommy's still on antibiotics, do make him finish the
   bottle, he takes it in Ribena. It's no good in orange, he
   spits it out. Remind me to give you Cathy's swimming
   things.

CATHY I did six strokes, didn't I Martin? Did I do a width?
   How many strokes is a length? How many miles is a

swimming pool? I'm going to take my bronze and silver and gold and diamond.

MARTIN Is Tommy still wetting the bed?

EDWARD Don't get angry with him about it.

MARTIN I just need to go to the launderette so I've got a spare sheet. Of course I don't get fucking angry, Eddy, for God's sake. I don't like to say he is my son but he is my son. I'm surprised I'm not wetting the bed myself.

CATHY I don't wet the bed ever. Do you wet the bed Martin?

MARTIN No.

CATHY You said you did.

Betty comes.

BETTY I do miss the sun living in England but today couldn't be more beautiful. You appreciate the weekend when you're working. Betty's been at work this week, Cathy. It's terribly tiring, Martin, I don't know how you've done it all these years. And the money, I feel like a child with the money, Clive always paid everything but I do understand it perfectly well. Look Cathy let me show you my money.

CATHY I'll count it. Let me count it. What's that?

BETTY Five pounds. Five and five is—?

CATHY One two three—

BETTY Five and five is ten, and five—

CATHY If I get it right can I have one?

EDWARD No you can't.

Cathy goes on counting the money.

BETTY I never like to say anything, Martin, or you'll think I'm being a mother-in-law.

EDWARD Which you are.

BETTY Thank you, Edward, I'm not talking to you. Martin, I think you're being wonderful. Vicky will come back. Just let her stay with Lin till she sorts herself out. It's very nice for a girl to have a friend; I had friends at school, that was very nice. But I'm sure Lin and Edward don't want her with them all the time. I'm not at all shocked that Lin and Edward aren't married and she already has a child, we all know first marriages don't always work out. But really Vicky must be in the way. And poor little Tommy. I hear he doesn't sleep properly and he's had a cough.

MARTIN No, he's fine, Betty, thank you.

CATHY My bed's horrible. I want to sleep in the big bed with Lin and Vicky and Eddy and I do get in if I've got a bad dream, and my bed's got a bump right in my back. I want to sleep in a tent.

BETTY Well Tommy has got a nasty cough, Martin, whatever you say.

EDWARD He's over that. He's got some medicine.

MARTIN He takes it in Ribena.

BETTY Well I'm glad to hear it. Look what a lot of money, Cathy, and I sit behind a desk of my own and I answer the telephone and keep the doctor's appointment book and it really is great fun.

CATHY Can we go camping, Martin, in a tent? We could take the Dead Hand Gang.

BETTY Not those big boys, Cathy? They're far too big and rough for you. They climb back into the park after dark. I'm sure mummy doesn't let you play with them, does she Edward? Well I don't know.

Ice cream bells.

CATHY Ice cream. Martin you promised. I'll have a double ninety nine. No I'll have a shandy lolly. Betty, you have a shandy lolly and I'll have a lick. No, you have a double ninety nine and I'll have the chocolate.

Martin, Cathy and Betty go, leaving Edward. Gerry comes.

GERRY Hello, Eddy. Thought I might find you here.

EDWARD Gerry.

GERRY Not working today then?

EDWARD I don't work here any more.

GERRY Your mum got you into a dark suit?

EDWARD No of course not. I'm on the dole. I am working, though, I do housework.

GERRY Whose wife are you now then?

EDWARD Nobody's. I don't think like that any more. I'm living with some women.

GERRY What women?

EDWARD It's my sister, Vic, and her lover. They go out to work and I look after the kids.

GERRY I thought for a moment you said you were living with women.

EDWARD We do sleep together, yes.

GERRY I was passing the park anyway so I thought I'd look in. I was in the sauna the other night and I saw someone who looked like you but it wasn't. I had sex with him anyway.

EDWARD I do go to the sauna sometimes.

Cathy comes, gives Edward an ice cream, goes.

GERRY I don't think I'd like living with children. They make a lot of noise don't they?

EDWARD I tell them to shut up and they shut up. I wouldn't want to leave them at the moment.

GERRY Look why don't we go for a meal sometime?

EDWARD Yes I'd like that.

Edward goes. Harry comes. Harry and Gerry pick each other up. They go off. Betty comes back.

BETTY No, the ice cream was my treat, Martin. Off you go. I'm going to have a quiet sit in the sun.

Maud comes.

MAUD Let Mrs. Saunders be a warning to you, Betty. I know what it is to be unprotected.

BETTY But mother, I have a job. I earn money.

MAUD I know we have our little differences but I always want what is best for you.

Ellen comes.

ELLEN Betty, what happens with a man?

BETTY You just keep still.

ELLEN And is it enjoyable? Don't forget me, Betty.

Maud and Ellen go.

BETTY I used to think Clive was the one who liked sex. But then I found I missed it. I used to touch myself when I was very little, I thought I'd invented something wonderful. I used to do it to go to sleep with or to cheer myself up, and one day it was raining and I was under the kitchen table, and my mother saw me with my hand under my dress rubbing away, and she dragged me out so quickly I hit my head and it bled and I was sick, and nothing was said, and I never did it again till this year. I thought if Clive wasn't looking at me there wasn't a person there. And one night in bed in my flat I was so frightened I started touching myself. I thought my hand might go through into space. I touched my face, it was there, my arm, my breast, and my hand went down where I thought it shouldn't, and I thought well there is somebody there. It felt very sweet, it was a feeling from very long ago, it was very soft, just barely touching, and I felt myself gathering together more and more and I felt angry with Clive and angry with my mother and I went on and on defying them, and there was this vast feeling growing in me and all round me and they couldn't stop me and no one could stop me and I was there and coming and coming. Afterwards I thought I'd betrayed Clive. My mother would kill me. But I felt triumphant because I was a separate person from them. And I cried because I didn't want to be. But I don't cry about it any more. Sometimes I do it three times in one night and it really is great fun.

Victoria and Lin come in.

VICTORIA So I said to the professor, I don't think this is an occasion for invoking the concept of structural causality —oh hello mummy.

BETTY I'm going to ask you a question, both of you. I have a little money from your grandmother. And the three of you are living in that tiny flat with two children. I wonder if we could get a house and all live in it together? It would give you more room.

VICTORIA But I'm going to Manchester anyway.

LIN We'd have a garden, Vicky.

BETTY You do seem to have such fun all of you.

VICTORIA I don't want to.

BETTY I didn't think you would.

LIN Come on, Vicky, she knows we sleep together, and Eddy.

BETTY I think I've known for quite a while but I'm not sure. I don't usually think about it, so I don't know if I know about it or not.

VICTORIA I don't want to live with my mother.

LIN Don't think of her as your mother, think of her as Betty.

VICTORIA But she thinks of herself as my mother.

BETTY I am your mother.

VICTORIA But mummy we don't even like each other.

BETTY We might begin to.

Cathy comes on howling with a nosebleed.

LIN Oh Cathy what happened?

BETTY She's been assaulted.

VICTORIA It's a nosebleed.

CATHY Took my ice cream.

LIN Who did?

CATHY Took my money.
    Martin comes.

MARTIN Is everything all right?

LIN I thought you were looking after her.

CATHY They hit me. I can't play. They said I'm a girl.

BETTY Those dreadful boys, the gang, the Dead Hand.

MARTIN What do you mean you thought I was looking after her?

LIN Last I saw her she was with you getting an ice cream. It's your afternoon.

MARTIN Then she went off to play. She goes off to play. You don't keep an eye on her every minute.

LIN She doesn't get beaten up when I'm looking after her.

CATHY Took my money.

MARTIN Why the hell should I look after your child anyway? I just want Tommy. Why should he live with you and Vicky all week?

LIN I don't mind if you don't want to look after her but don't say you will and then this happens.

VICTORIA When I go to Manchester everything's going to be different anyway, Lin's staying here, and you're staying here, we're all going to have to sit down and talk it through.

MARTIN I'd really enjoy that.

CATHY Hit me on the face.

LIN You were the one looking after her and look at her now, that's all.

MARTIN I've had enough of you telling me.

LIN Yes you know it all.

MARTIN Now stop it. I work very hard at not being like this, I could do with some credit.

LIN Ok you're quite nice, try and enjoy it. Don't make me sorry for you, Martin, it's hard for me too. We've better things to do than quarrel. I've got to go and sort those little bastards out for a start. Where are they, Cathy?

CATHY Don't kill them, mum, hit them. Give them a nosebleed, mum.

Lin goes.

VICTORIA Tommy's asleep in the pushchair. We'd better wake him up or he won't sleep tonight.

MARTIN Sometimes I keep him up watching television till he falls asleep on the sofa so I can hold him. Come on, Cathy, we'll get another ice cream.

CATHY Chocolate sauce and nuts.

VICTORIA Betty, would you like an ice cream?

BETTY No thank you, the cold hurts my teeth, but what a nice thought, Vicky, thank you.

Vicky goes. Betty alone. Gerry comes.

BETTY I think you used to be Edward's flatmate.

GERRY You're his mother. He's talked about you.

BETTY Well never mind. Children are always wrong about their parents. It's great problem knowing where to live and who to share with. I live by myself just now.

GERRY Good. So do I. You can do what you like.

BETTY I don't really know what I like.

GERRY You'll soon find out.

BETTY What do you like?

GERRY Waking up at four in the morning.

BETTY I like listening to music in bed and sometimes for supper I just have a big piece of bread and dip it in very hot lime pickle. So you don't get lonely by yourself? Perhaps you have a lot of visitors. I've been thinking I should have some visitors, I could give a little dinner party. Would you come? There wouldn't just be bread and lime pickle.

GERRY Thank you very much.

BETTY Or don't wait to be asked to dinner. Just drop in informally. I'll give you the address shall I? I don't usually give strange men my address but then you're not a strange man, you're a friend of Edward's. I suppose I seem a different generation to you but you are older than Edward. I was married for so many years it's quite hard to know how to get acquainted. But if there isn't a right way to do things you have to invent one. I always thought my mother was far too old to be attractive but when you get to an age yourself it feels quite different.

GERRY I think you could be quite attractive.

BETTY If what?

GERRY If you stop worrying.

BETTY I think when I do more about things I worry about them less. So perhaps you could help me do more.

GERRY I might be going to live with Edward again.

BETTY That's nice, but I'm rather surprised if he wants to share a flat. He's rather involved with a young woman he lives with, or two young women, I don't understand Edward but never mind.

GERRY I'm very involved with him.

BETTY I think Edward did try to tell me once but I didn't listen. So what I'm being told now is that Edward is 'gay' is that right? And you are too. And I've being making rather a fool of myself. But Edward does also sleep with women.

GERRY He does, yes, I don't.

BETTY Well people always say it's the mother's fault but I don't intend to start blaming myself. He seems perfectly happy.

GERRY I could still come and see you.

BETTY So you could, yes. I'd like that. I've never tried to pick up a man before.

GERRY Not everyone's gay.

BETTY No, that's lucky isn't it.

Gerry goes. Clive comes.

CLIVE You are not that sort of woman, Betty. I can't believe you are. I can't feel the same about you as I did. And Africa is to be communist I suppose. I used to be proud to be British. There was a high ideal. I came out onto the verandah and looked at the stars.

Clive goes. Betty from Act 1 comes. Betty and Betty embrace.